T0311684

Autism Friendly Cities

Autism Friendly Cities
How to Develop an Inclusive Community

Jennifer Percival, Ph.D., CRC

Routledge
Taylor & Francis Group

A PRODUCTIVITY PRESS BOOK

Cover Illustrator: The cover was illustrated by Andrew Blitman, an artist with autism, who resides in South Florida. Andrew earned a Master's Degree in Marine Conservation Science & Policy from the University of Miami. He served on the UM-NSU Center for Autism and Related Disabilities constituency board from 2011 to 2017. Andrew currently works as a painter, tutor, and mentor, and has served on the Els Center for Autism advisory board since 2018. He is the author of a memoir about his life, and several works of poetry. You can find out more about Andrew by visiting his website at andrewblitman.com.

First published 2022
by Routledge
605 Third Avenue, New York, NY 10158

and by Routledge
2 Park Square, Milton Park, Abingdon, Oxon, OX14 4RN

Routledge is an imprint of the Taylor & Francis Group, an informa business

© 2022 Jennifer Percival

The right of Jennifer Percival to be identified as author of this work has been asserted by her in accordance with sections 77 and 78 of the Copyright, Designs and Patents Act 1988.
All rights reserved. No part of this book may be reprinted or reproduced or utilised in any form or by any electronic, mechanical, or other means, now known or hereafter invented, including photocopying and recording, or in any information storage or retrieval system, without permission in writing from the publishers.

Trademark notice: Product or corporate names may be trademarks or registered trademarks, and are used only for identification and explanation without intent to infringe.

ISBN: 9781032028231 (hbk)
ISBN: 9781032028224 (pbk)
ISBN: 9781003185369 (ebk)

DOI: 10.4324/9781003185369

Typeset in Garamond
by Deanta Global Publishing Services, Chennai, India

For Debbie Majors

Contents

Acknowledgments

Memories of our lives, of our works and our deeds
will continue in others.

– Rosa Parks

This book would not have been possible without the visionaries who created the Autism Friendly Cities movement. They saw obstacles to access and inclusion, and were dedicated to adapting policies, practices, and perceptions in their communities to create change. The person who took on that challenge, and who inspired this book, is Debbie Majors. As the ADA (Americans with Disabilities Act) Coordinator for the City of Boynton Beach, located in South Florida, she engaged with the process of building an Autism Friendly City.

While applying new concepts across an entire community, she climbed the hill of a significant learning curve and found herself in a place no other city leader had been. This did not discourage her. It further motivated her to conceive new ideas that were innovative and inventive, developing solutions and solving problems. Debbie recognized and confronted not only the challenges faced by residents with autism but also those barriers that people with a variety of disabilities were experiencing. Using the available resources and crafting some that didn't previously exist, she put together a team and developed an neurodiverse and inclusive community. There are not enough words of appreciation to thank her for her courage, conviction, and perseverance.

Debbie Majors was the originator of this movement in my region, and she gathered help and support along the way, utilizing partnerships to transform her city. As a member of Debbie's team, I had the opportunity to know those who contributed to the process, and I thank them for their enthusiasm and resolve. These dedicated and talented people at the City of Boynton Beach, include Stephanie Soplop, the Recreation Manager (and new ADA Coordinator), and Ted Goodenough, the ADA Coordinator Assistant. The Inclusion Team, which consisted of representatives from many local human services and disability-related agencies and organizations, provided invaluable expertise. The city leadership, including Mayor Steven Grant and the city commissioners, helped sustain and support this effort over the years. The City of Boynton Beach serves as a model Autism Friendly City, thanks to Debbie Majors and her team of public servants that worked diligently to improve the quality of life for people with autism.

Florida Atlantic University's Center for Autism and Related Disabilities (FAU CARD) was central to the Autism Friendly Cities movement. Executive Director, Dr. Jack Scott, and Director, Dr. Maryellen Quinn-Lunny, were instrumental in advocating for this program, and they encouraged my ongoing work with the City of Boynton Beach and other local municipalities. FAU CARD's team of Clinical Specialists contributed their expertise through training and consultation to the City of Boynton Beach and to cities across the region. The University of South Florida's CARD Center was influential in developing an Autism Friendly Business program, which the FAU CARD program was modelled after. Their initiative in this area created the foundation needed to support the growth of the Autism Friendly Cities movement to a national stage.

As I wrote this book, my family, friends, and colleagues, were extremely supportive. Jeremy and EmJ, my children, you bring light to my world and inspire me every day. My parents, Ellen and Jerry, and Don and Susan, you encourage my work and understand my drive to try and make the world a better place. My brother Brian, I am thankful that you ensure there is always a bit of logic and reasoning in my universe. Erica, my closest lifelong friend, for over 40 years you've been just a phone call away and are ready to lend an ear on both the wonderful and the challenging days. There is no greater kindness. For all of the love in my life that lifts me up and reminds me why my words matter, I thank you.

Author Bio

Jennifer Percival, Ph.D., CRC

Dr. Jennifer Percival is Assistant Director of Florida Atlantic University's Center for Autism and Related Disabilities (FAU CARD). She holds a Doctorate from FAU in Educational Leadership and Research Methodology with a research area of Disability Studies. She is a Nationally Certified Rehabilitation Counselor (CRC), published author, and expert on inclusion, disability employment strategies, and the transition experience. Jennifer is a sought-after speaker and consultant on program development.

Jennifer is the founder of the Autism Friendly Cities and Autism Friendly Business programs at FAU CARD. She is the creator of the world's only Autism Friendly Cities Institute. Jennifer is an award-winning researcher in disability studies. She participates on national and regional boards, work groups, and committees that guide cities and business through the Autism Friendly process. Jennifer serves on the Royal Caribbean International Autism Advisory Board, the CareerSource Palm Beach County Youth Employment Board, the City of Boynton Beach Inclusion Team, Palm Beach County's Special Needs Advisory Council, and the Palm Beach Council for In Transition Youth. Jennifer was the 2019 Florida Graduate Research Symposium second place state-wide winner for her dissertation research. She was the State of Florida's Workforce System's Barbara Griffin Workforce Excellence Award winner in 2017, FAU's Lifelong Learning Society Lunafest Scholarship recipient in 2017, and FAU's College of Education North Campus Student of the Year in 2016.

Prior to working at FAU CARD, Jennifer divided her career between the Florida Department of Education's Division of Vocational Rehabilitation, and the Florida Department of Children and Families. Jennifer is a community leader who develops infrastructure through her work with collaborations and regional planning, while assisting professionals and individuals with program improvement and strategic implementation.

* The views and opinions expressed in this book belong solely to the author, and do not represent those of FAU, FAU CARD, or FLDOE.

Introduction

How wonderful it is that nobody need wait a single moment before starting to improve the world.

– Anne Frank

The United States Center for Disease Control reports that 1 in 44 individuals are diagnosed with an autism spectrum disorder (2021). This is an incredibly high number. In the United Kingdom, the prevalence is 1 in 57 children has autism. The World Health Organization indicates that globally 1 in 270 people is diagnosed with an autism spectrum disorder. From both a national and global perspective, these numbers are staggering. In a city of 50,000 people, approximately 1,135 people will have autism. When you add a zero, a city of 500,000 people has 11,350 individuals who live with autism. Even in a small town, you will, without a doubt, have residents in your local community who are on the autism spectrum. Those residents will vary in age, ethnicity, and socioeconomic level. They will be children, adults, and everything in between. There will also be others who are touched by autism: a grandparent, a neighbor, and people who care for, support, and love people with autism. Whether you are interacting directly with a person who has autism or working with their family members and loved ones, people with autism, and those in their support system, will be impacted by the choices you make in your city. Your decisions, as a city employee, city manager, or city leader, will influence lives. Even things you may believe are insignificant, like the design of your website, to the knowledge of the person sitting at the front desk in your welcome center, from the training of your camp counselors, to the strategies used by your basketball coaches, the lens through which you choose to work and view your city has the power to shape the lives of the residents in the community that you serve.

Who Is This Book For?

If you work in a city, municipality, town, county, or village, then this book is for you. Are you an HR Manager? A Commissioner? A Mayor? This book can help you successfully fulfill those roles. Are you a recreation leader or program director? Are you an event coordinator? Do you contribute to the construction or development of public spaces? Then this book can provide you guidance. Are you a professional in human services or social care? Do you advise city staff or public works? Do you train their swim teachers or dance instructors? This book can help you help others. This book is for anyone who works in a public position where they come into contact with the community. It is for those who serve residents in various ways, those who teach them, design for them, provide assistance to them, create spaces, develop programs, or coordinate events. Most importantly, this book is for anyone whose goal is to facilitate an inclusionary perspective for their community, and for those who strive to have a better understanding of autism, along with the desire to develop specific tools, methods, and an approach to support a neurodiverse society.

This book is also intended for readers interested in inclusion, for students, and academics, as well as for general readers. Strategies learned may be applied to environments in classrooms, businesses, or various organizational settings. For an academic audience, those studying urban planning, organizational leadership, special education, diversity, or disability studies will find this information useful and practical. Individuals with autism are invited to utilize this book to share with their own city staff and leaders as they encounter challenges and wish to offer options to those who develop and deliver programming and public projects. This book was written in the United States, but the principles can be applied internationally. Over the past several years, while doing this work, city representatives from around the world have reached out to me as they looked for guidance and support while creating Autism Friendly and inclusive communities. I've consulted with city staff and teams from across the United States, Northern Ireland, the United Kingdom, and Russia. No matter where you reside, or what you call your town, village, or community, there will be people with autism living there who deserve access to all that your city offers. Even if it is just one person with autism or neurodifference, they deserve to be included, accepted, and celebrated as part of their community, which makes it your responsibility to have an understanding of their needs.

What about Us?

The Autism Friendly Cities movement started with the goal of improving access to city services for residents with autism. However, it was quickly learned that education and resources were needed for communities to embrace this initiative and develop innovative and effective ways to open doors and truly enrich the resident experience for individuals with autism and their families. Cities also needed to enhance how they've been interpreting and adhering to the local and national laws that support access and that are designed to improve the way individuals with disabilities interact with their city. Despite laws such as the Americans with Disabilities Act (ADA), people with autism and neurodiversity encounter challenges and difficulty connecting with all that is provided by the government in the location where they live. These offerings range from services to classes, and camps to concerts, as cities facilitate useful and broad services, even to utilities or necessities like requesting a permit or paying a water bill. While experiences can vary from program to program or place to place, neurodiverse people should not run into barriers when they want to attend a local sporting event, participate in a recreation class, or even engage in something as simple as playing at the park. There should not be obstacles to partaking in and enjoying these activities and events or securing public assistance. Every person, regardless of developmental or neurological ability, should be able to utilize and have access to what every other resident, community member, and tax payer expects from their city.

The concept of inclusion is not complex, but it does require a greater understanding of the lived experience of residents in order to fully remove barriers to access and to include them in your city with equity and equality. Cities must be radically honest about the ways in which they design their systems, and recognize that they may not truly be open to all. When planning communities, inclusion must be more than just an idea and needs to be considered across every aspect of a city, from the town hall to the website, from a musical event to summer camp, and from an art program to the nature preserve. Our towns and municipalities offer so much to the public, and they must be a place where everyone has the opportunity and the support available to participate. To be able to engage with what is available just outside one's own doorstep, without being excluded or isolated from the practical, social, recreational, and educational aspects of the community, contributes to a sense of belonging and a meaningful life.

What about Others?

Throughout the years of doing this work, I've learned that when you design for a small percentage of the population, you frequently reach many others, often having a direct impact on the people who are outside of your original purpose. For example, when designing inclusive signage, which is extremely visual, you are supporting access for a person with autism and also providing an accommodation for people who may not read, for those who are nonverbal, for people who only read other languages, or for those with a variety of disabilities. When asking yourself if your efforts will have a broad reach, consider this lens: when you intend to help a few, you will likely help many.

It is important to note that this book, and the Autism Friendly movement, is a work in progress. As strategies are developed and successes achieved, more approaches will be added and shared over time. Other books may be needed in the future, as even this text cannot possibly be all-encompassing. For example, this book will only touch on and not delve into information for first responders. Those in law enforcement, firefighting, emergency medical, and on rapid response teams require highly specific and in-depth training that goes beyond the scope of what can be offered in these pages.. While emergency registries, and other mechanisms of support, are discussed in this book, specialized information and education is recommended for first response professionals. There may also be other resources and trainings your city needs to address the needs of individuals with a variety of disabilities, or for circumstances or settings not reviewed here. This book will provide you the framework, general information, and strategies to develop an Autism Friendly City. It is a place to begin.

What I Hope You Gain from These Pages

The purpose of this book is to broaden your views of the people with autism who reside, work, play, and live in your city. My vision is that this text helps you better understand what they need in order to be included and celebrated in the spaces and programs you create. At the very least, my goal is to help you shift your perspective and to encourage you to do things differently than before. As you go about your day-to-day job, consider what you are creating and how it can be modified, even just a little, to be a more accessible experience for people with autism. When you shift even the small things, opportunities open up in ways they never did before. Something you may have thought insignificant, like adding visuals to your city's app, or turning the house lights up during a theater performance, including a child in a dance class, or displaying the art of a young adult with autism, has the power to be profoundly meaningful. It is in this slightly different way of looking at the world and modifying your way of work which can become transformative to the life of a person with autism. When you hesitate or feel uncertain, Margaret Mead offers some advice, sharing to "Never doubt that a small group of thoughtful, committed citizens can change the world; indeed, it's the only thing that ever has."

Please feel free to contact me to ask questions or seek consultation. I can be reached at drjenniferpercival@gmail.com or www.jenniferpercival.com.

THE WHY

Why Are We Here?
Why Does This Matter?

1

> When I was young, my ambition was to be one of
> the people who made a difference in this world. My
> hope is to leave the world a little better for having
> been there.
>
> **– Jim Henson**

During the first year I offered trainings on how to be Autism
Friendly, I did not include a PowerPoint slide on why the
training was important or why I was there. In my naïveté,
I thought it was obvious. I knew that as a society we were
not doing enough. I knew that we were not doing the right
things. I figured everyone else realized that as well, and that
was why we were in a training room learning about what else
could be done. I was wrong. Most people I came into contact
with didn't understand that there was an issue. They thought
that large bathroom stalls and up-front parking were meeting
or even exceeding ADA requirements and making their city

DOI: 10.4324/9781003185369-1

accessible. What they didn't recognize was that they were just scratching the surface of inclusion and disregarding entire segments of the neurodiverse population.

One afternoon I was speaking to a room of employees who worked for a government entity, a few who apparently were mandated to be in my training, and were not participating voluntarily. Three slides into my presentation, one of them raised a hand, and with a spitfire attitude, demanded to know why this information was necessary, and why she herself had to sit through it. I was surprised and a bit taken aback by the question. Didn't everyone want to make the world more inclusive? Wasn't everyone interested in how they could do their job better and in ways that opened doors to members of their community? My utopian ideals were challenged and I had to develop an on-the-spot response to her question. As I explained to her, I will describe to you in this section: why are we here learning about this group of people and what their needs are? Why does being Autism Friendly matter?

Why Am I Here?

A mother called me one day at work and asked me about summer camps options for her son with autism. We talked about various programs, including a soccer camp that was being offered by the city she lived in. After she reached out to them, she called me back. The program did not accept children with autism. She was saddened, frustrated, and discouraged. Why was her child not allowed to attend the same camp that the neighborhood children went to? Why wasn't he allowed to play soccer with his friends that he attended school with? How could that be? They didn't give the mother a thorough explanation, simply that they weren't equipped for her son to attend. At that point, I picked up the phone and called the city. Their reason for not including this child was that the

camp was not prepared to serve a child with "extra needs."
For me, that was not a reasonable response.

A young adult I was working with emailed me that he had
recently moved out of this mother's home and into an apart-
ment of his own for the first time. He was excited about this
step towards more independence in his life, but there was
some confusion over who was supposed to pay the utility
bills. He was told by the landlord that he needed to switch
the water bill into his name. To accomplish this, he went to
the local city office, which, he confirmed via phone, was the
correct location, but when he arrived, there were many doors
to the building, little signage, and once inside, he didn't know
where to go or who to talk to. After finally finding a staff person to ask for help, he was told to sign into a computer in the
lobby and wait. When he approached the computer, there was
a login screen with no directions indicating what to do. He
was so overwhelmed and stressed by the process, he decided
to go home instead, not transferring the utility account into his
name.

An adult with autism came to my office to discuss employment options. She was interested in working as an art class
assistant. We talked about the job tasks for that type of work
and decided to look online for local open positions. We
found one in a neighboring city, where they were hiring part
time. She completed the application, submitted a resume, and
was later contacted for an interview. During the interview,
she struggled with eye contact and was required to verbally
answer questions that she'd never heard or seen before. She
felt stressed during the experience and did not clearly express
herself. As a result, she did not adequately show her talents
or explain her experience and ultimately did not obtain the
position.

A group of families who have children with autism get
together once a month for social experiences. They decided
that for their winter outing they would visit the Santa Claus

housed in a special area of the park in their city. They tried going during a weekday at a quiet time, but they ended up having a negative experience anyway. One of the mothers called me to share what happened. She said that the parking area was very near a lake and there were no barriers to keep the children from running toward the water. In their excitement to see Santa, one of the younger children ran from the car and had to be detoured from the water area. When they were inside the building, the decorations were beautiful, but the space, which was mostly wooden, was loud, echoed, and was filled with people. The line to see Santa was over 20 children long, and the wait was over an hour. There were no activities to do in line, and most of the children in their group were unable to wait that long. They were also overstimulated by the environment, and many children sadly went home without visiting Santa.

These stories, these experiences, of individuals with autism and their families, are frustrating, discouraging, and heartbreaking. It is essential that everyone has the chance to be part of the community: for a young person to go to summer camp, an adult to independently manage his bills, an individual to have a fair shot at a job, and a child to have a magical holiday experience. With a few small changes, a little education, and some thought, a city has the ability to include everyone in the opportunities they offer. The reason I do this work is to ensure you have the information and resources necessary to take action and make choices that have the potential to be life-changing for the residents of your community.

Chapter 1

The Good, the Bad, and the PR Nightmares

All the adversity I've had in my life, all my troubles
and obstacles, have strengthened me … you may not
realize it when it happens, but a kick in the teeth
may be the best thing in the world for you.

– Walt Disney

There are definitely cities, organizations, and groups out there
that are doing a good job of creating accessible and inclusive
environments, but there are also those that profoundly fail.
This chapter will review what happens when you support
expansive access and inclusion, and when you lack action in
this area. It will also share stories of what happens when a
group is required to be reactive due to a negative situation or
because environments were created through a narrow lens. It
is likely that some of the leaders who will pick up this book
are doing so because they are managing an incident or issue
and are looking to rectify the situation. Perhaps they feel they
did everything right, but for some reason something still went
wrong. Or, they did nothing at all, and are now being forced

DOI: 10.4324/9781003185369-2

to address the consequences of that inaction. This chapter will showcase what happens when your approach is one of neurodiversity and inclusion. It will also examine potential issues when accessibility is limited and barriers remain, because the needs of specific populations are not considered. This section will teach you how to break down your organization's needs, to help you gain insight, and to begin to shift the perspective. It is also for those in a situation where they need to 'right the ship'.

The Good

There is a 30-second video I show when I train people on the Autism Friendly movement. The clip is a demonstration of low budget, high impact return on investment. In the video, a young boy with autism dreams of surfing. He is nonverbal and has high support needs, meaning he requires 24-hour supervision for safety and direct assistance for activities of daily living. He indicates to his parents, many times, through watching videos, gestures, and mirroring, that he wants to have a surfing experience. For the family vacation, they went on a cruise, and the ship had a surfing pool onboard. The pool utilizes high-powered water jets to simulate waves. Surfing, without assistance, would require abilities that this child did not have, and additional safety measures would need to be in place. Luckily, this cruise line was Autism Friendly, and they were able to make several small modifications, such as turning down the water pressure to make the waves less demanding, adding a specialized life jacket to the child, and increasing the staff, where one lifeguard helped move the child into the water, and another was already in the water and able to hold the child on a boogie board throughout the experience. The cruise staff involved had also received basic training about autism. These few adjustments, which required little time and minimal cost, allowed this child and the family to have an experience that fulfilled on a dream. The video has been shared widely, and not only do viewers frequently cry at the beauty of the moment, but they also admire the practices of the business and those involved in supporting this child's experience.

The Bad

Unfortunately, there are many stories to share about what happens when things go wrong. There are news reports and articles that detail horrifying accounts of people with autism being so misunderstood that what might have been solved with a simple intervention or accommodation turned into a significant problem, or even a tragedy. There are situations when families tried to connect with a city for resources or services and were turned away, resulting in exclusion and even isolation, leaving an individual with no options or recourse. Other experiences, where it seemed like there could be a simple fix, or a strategy utilized, created negative moments for families, and in turn, cities. These adverse circumstances have the power to significantly negatively impact residents and can easily turn into legal and Public Relations nightmares for a city.

PR Nightmares

We've all watched the news and heard about a city, town, or company that is being publicly admonished for making a poor decision. When there are negative incidents that occur, especially if a person with a disability is harmed or experiences discrimination, the public responds by making a judgment about that organization. This may mean loss of resident engagement, economic downturn, or even in-person protests and outcries on social media. The image of the city becomes tarnished or tainted, and it can take years to reestablish trust with the community.

Education is at the core of the solution to PR nightmares, as both a preventative and a restorative method. It could be that an employee simply didn't have the knowledge or expertise to handle a situation appropriately, and that is what caused an issue to occur. Or, a staff person did have information but did not have the know-how to implement their understanding of ways to support a person in the moment. Either a lack of thorough staff training, the need for more resources, or how an organization's values may not align with serving the entire community with inclusivity can cause these situations to occur. Once these incidents happen, and are made public, a city, is forced to do damage control. This is often handled by back-tracking and promising to train or retrain employees, or to add additional components to professional development curriculum that simply wasn't there in the first place. Frequently, this also includes a change of branding or a new values' statement that helps to cover up the problem, with the goal of resetting the tone for the future and calming the public's response. Even with these fixes, the reputation of an organization can be tarnished long-term. Being proactive to prevent a problem is much more effective than managing it after the fact. Being exceptionally honest and genuine when conducting a self-analysis of the way in which your city functions, where there are strengths and weaknesses and how improvements may be made to reduce barriers and increase access, is necessary to develop a plan to move your city toward being neurodiverse and Autism Friendly. I suggest that this is the place to begin your journey. Start here, with reflection, analysis, and a goal to gain insight. Discussions with your team can be conducted in many ways: individually, in groups, managerial levels, departments, or by utilizing focus groups. Set the tone of the space to encourage staff, to share their experiences and express their feelings about your city. The set of prompts, Reflection: The Good and the Bad is designed to provide a framework, start the self-evaluation process, and encourage conversation.

*Reflection: The Good and the Bad

Utilize the following prompts as conversation starters:

- Share a positive story about a time a person with autism had a successful experience participating in a city program or service.
- Discuss an uplifting personal experience of working directly with a person with autism in your capacity as a city employee.
- If there are autism-specific programs or events in your city, are they inclusive, or do they segregate people with autism into groups where they are only with others who also have autism? (for example, sensory-friendly story hour) Reflect on how this may or may not be a useful experience to offer.
- Has a person with autism reported an experience where they felt excluded or encountered barriers to services or programs in your city?
- Are there city staff who have requested to restrict program attendance to children without autism or disabilities?
- Have there been complaints by parents or families about limited inclusion opportunities or barriers to accessing services?
- Are all of the programs you offer open to anyone with any level of need or support? If not, what are your limitations, and why?
- Has there been a negative incident related to a person with autism due to an interaction with city staff? If so, what steps were taken after the incident to remedy the situation? Did those steps resolve the issue, or were they a temporary fix? If not, are you concerned this type of incident may happen in your city?
- Has there been an incident in your city related to a person with autism that resulted in negative media coverage? If so, how did your city handle that situation?

A Dialogue: DEIA

As we discuss our experiences and begin to develop a lens as an approach that promotes inclusion, we must discuss DEIA (Diversity, Equity, Inclusion, and Accessibility). DEIA is a practice and way of work that addresses inequity. In 2021, via Executive Order 13985, the United States federal government issued the following definitions for these terms:

- The term "diversity" means the practice of including the many communities, identities, races, ethnicities, backgrounds, abilities, cultures, and beliefs of the American people, including underserved communities.
- The term "equity" means the consistent and systematic fair, just, and impartial treatment of all individuals, including individuals who belong to underserved communities that have been denied such treatment.
- The term "inclusion" means the recognition, appreciation, and use of the talents and skills of employees of all backgrounds.
- The term "accessibility" means the design, construction, development, and maintenance of facilities, information and communication technology, programs, and services so that all people, including people with disabilities, can fully and independently use them. Accessibility includes the provision of accommodations and modifications to ensure equal access to employment and participation in activities for people with disabilities, the reduction or elimination of physical and attitudinal barriers to equitable opportunities, a commitment to ensuring that people with disabilities can independently access every outward-facing and internal activity or electronic space, and the pursuit of best practices such as universal design.

The practice of DEIA is being integrated into many organizations, workplaces, and mission statements. This incorporation of DEIA can be discussed in your city, as an aspect of strategic planning, training curriculum, work practice, and as a lens of doing business internally and when public facing. An organization called Disability:IN, which offers training and a network to organizations that support inclusive business practices, talks about their use of a DEI index as an instrument. They explain their process: "The Disability Equality Index (DEI) is a comprehensive benchmarking tool that helps companies build a roadmap of measurable, tangible actions that they can take to achieve disability inclusion and equality. Each company receives a score, on a scale of zero (0) to 100, with those earning 80 and above recognized as Best Places to Work for Disability Inclusion." When approaching DEIA it is essential to begin with an uncompromising level of self-assessment, personally and globally. Be committed to creating safe spaces for difficult discussions and meaningful problem solving, where every voice is heard. Thoughtful conversations are needed when asking yourself, your leaders, and your residents about their experience of working and living in your city.

Consider the Needs of Your City

Assessment is the first step toward building capacity. Begin by conducting an internal evaluation of your city's DEIA practices and philosophy, through an autism and disability lens. Is your city staff diverse? Do you have people with autism working for your city? Is your city equitable? When offering services to your residents, are people with autism or related disabilities treated the same way as residents without disabilities? Explore the ways you embrace those in your town that are autistic, and consider the level to which they are, or are not, being included. As a more global question, reflect on every aspect of your city, and ask yourself if all opportunities are accessible to every person. If not, are you committed to making changes in both design and execution? Does your city celebrate and embrace neurodiversity? What don't you know? What do you feel is missing? Is your team open to change? These are the places to begin. Utilize the previous questions and the following brainstorming work-sheet as an informal evaluation.

*Brainstorm: Evaluate Your City

Begin with either a specific department or a global overview of your city. Kick the tires and have a look under the hood. Evaluate and assess. Discuss what you know, consider what you don't know, and start to have the difficult conversations about what needs to be done. These questions will help you initiate a dialogue.

■ Do you know how many individuals living in your city are on the autism spectrum? If you don't have this data, how can you obtain it?

■ Are you aware of organizations and agencies in your city that support people with autism? If so, which ones?

■ What internal policies or initiatives are currently in place to support the inclusion of people with autism?

■ If no policies are in place, what is your most pressing concern related to autism and inclusion? What needs to be addressed first?

■ Have city staff ever received any training about people with disabilities and what their needs might be? If so, which staff, and were the takeaways implemented? Were any trainings specific to the needs of autistic or neurodiverse people?

■ What strategies are you currently using to support accessibility for people with autism? (i.e., visual supports, social stories)

■ How many city employees work directly with children or adults with autism in any capacity through city offerings?

■ Are programs that fall under the city or facilitated through contractors taught by people who are knowledgeable about autism?

■ Is there anyone with autism who is on an advisory team, commission board, or work group in your city? How are people with autism represented?

■ What worries you the most about not being an Autism Friendly City? Are there city staff or leaders that are resistant to your city being Autism Friendly?

■ Have you experienced a situation where a person with autism was excluded or was unable to participate due to the required supports not being in place?

■ If you could make one change immediately, to increase neurodiverse practice in your city, what would that change be, and why?

Chapter 2

Recruiting Others

> If solutions within the system are so impossible to
> find, then maybe we should change the system itself.
>
> **– Greta Thunberg**

If you are the designated disability manager, ADA coordinator,
HR specialist, or the one who decided to pick up this book
in the hope that your city might be willing to embrace a new
initiative, you may need to help your colleagues or leaders
commit to the idea of making your city Autism Friendly. After
working through the evaluation process, the next steps are
to present your findings and utilize models and successes to
guide others to visualize and understand why this initiative is
important and how it can impact the lives of residents. Autism
Friendly Cities exist to improve accessibility, increase autism
awareness, expand community inclusion, and enhance opportunities. It may be surprising that certain members of your
city team might need to be nudged into supporting the Autism
Friendly approach. While it is a strong program that is socially
responsible and grounded in human rights, you may have
some colleagues who are hesitant. This section will support

DOI: 10.4324/9781003185369-3

you in encouraging others in your city to commit to the project and the process.

Who Is at the Forefront of This Movement?

My work in the Autism Friendly Cities movement was launched from an Autism Friendly Business initiative. That project had similar goals of access and inclusion. It was the City of Boynton Beach, a local town, in South Florida, that heard about what was being taught to businesses and how they were implementing strategies. They reached out to me to ask if the same principles could be applied to their structure. After an initial consultation and a discussion of how the Autism Friendly lens could inspire leaders to be more intentionally neurodiverse, specifically for people with autism, we agreed to talk about how to collaborate. Debbie Majors, the ADA Coordinator at the City of Boynton Beach, was driven to improve the city for neurodiverse individuals and was committed to creating practical but innovative ways to address the solvable problems while enhancing the lives of people who need support, and also broaden the reach of the city.

Over several years of hard work, what the City of Boynton Beach developed is nothing short of extraordinary. They started with education and training, brought in experts who made up their Inclusion Team, implemented strategies, and developed a support structure. Then they expanded the initiative to first responders, the hiring process, HR practices, mentoring, large events, park redesign, construction, way-finding, inclusive summer camps, children's programming, a business cooperative, art expos, and staff development which embraced this way of work, ultimately creating an inclusive city.

What Is the Time Commitment?

The time commitment to become Autism Friendly is dependent on the size of your city and the level which your team decides to engage with the process. If your city has minimal resources to dedicate to this initiative but wants to begin in a smaller way there are a couple of options. One is to pick a single department or program, such as a youth athletic department, and work through the steps to make it Autism Friendly. On this path the time required is reduced, and the city staff who are already working with children may bring some knowledge of autism and new strategies which can be easily incorporated. The second option is to create your Inclusion Team. Reach out to an autism expert in your area and ask for feedback on their perception of accessibility and neurodiversity in your city. Work with them to connect you with other agencies and disability programs, which will help you develop your contacts. If your city is willing to take this on, the majority of the required time commitment is for training city staff across departments, as well as possibly creating a position, partial position, or designee that serves as the facilitator and coordinator of your Autism Friendly program. Once your city begins the process, you will start to experience success and recognize the significance of the impact. It is often easier to encourage stakeholders to be committed to inclusion once they have a direct and practical understanding of how and why it is important. Moving the idea from concept to reality can be motivating, and using the approach of starting on the smaller scale, where leaders can plainly see the impact, while only utilizing minimal resources, can be effective. It is important to at least begin where you are, with what you have, because it is the starting that matters.

How Do We Pay for This?

Many of the strategies discussed in this book come at little
to no cost. For example, creating visual supports can be as
simple as using your computer software and printing on paper
then posting the visual. Additional expense might occur as
you take the process to the next level, but can still happen
with little cost, such as framing and hanging a visual support
in an inexpensive picture frame or a plastic stand. Another
way of keeping costs down is to use items that you already
own and that are part of the space. For example, if you have
a television that is in your city lobby, adding information and
visual supports that are Autism Friendly as scrolling slides
might be a no-cost solution.

There are times when financial resources are needed, and
most often this is in covering the salary for the hours required
for training, development, and implementation. For some, it
may be easy to incorporate these aspects as a part of their job
requirements. Training, for example, can be included in the
hiring and onboarding process for new staff. There may be
instances, however, when a task is slightly outside the scope
of some of your staff's responsibilities, and funding their time
to complete the assignment might have a small cost.

Larger financial commitments might include purchasing
furniture to redesign a physical space, or adding items like
a low sensory tent during an event. Other options that will
have a significant expense are projects on a large scale, like
constructing a playground or building, or redesigning a natural area. However, when these additions or modifications
are done as part of a conversion or maintenance, it is easier
to incorporate strategies at that time and receive input from
experts as part of the design phase, potentially saving costs
down the line. For example, if your city is going through

redevelopment or new construction, it is useful to bring in your Inclusion Team during the planning process so that it is more cost-friendly to incorporate strategies and spaces upfront versus creating additions afterward.

There are some practical and innovative ways to cover costs for the Autism Friendly initiative. There are cities that reach out to private funding sources, foundations, or apply for grants. Many national and international programs offer funds in the form of neighborhood or community project assistance. Another way that financial resources can be located is to look at your city budget and evaluate if any funds can be real-located. For example, the City of Boynton Beach decided to utilize some of the income from the parking tickets that are issued to people who illegally park in disabled parking spaces. This was an ingenious idea, because it redirected money they collected when the rights of people with disabilities were violated and they brought it back to the community the spaces were intended to serve.

Some cities also demonstrate their commitment to being Autism Friendly by hiring an ADA Specialist or Inclusion Coordinator. Sometimes these are full-time positions that cover an entire city, or the job tasks are incorporated into other roles, perhaps for a certain number of specified hours per week. Having this type of person on staff at your city, with job responsibilities that include maintaining updated laws and pol-icies, facilitating the Inclusion Team, as well as working closely with residents, can be an excellent opportunity for your city to ensure being neurodiverse is a long-term plan and not just a short-term project. It also demonstrates a city's commitment to have a dedicated person to work through the initial stages of becoming an Autism Friendly City. These types of positions are typically paid for utilizing government funds, as the ser-vice is provided directly to city residents.

Economic Development

A consideration when deciding if your city should become Autism Friendly is economic development. When cities are open to all, their reach is wider, and their interaction with residents is more meaningful. Residents may feel a stronger level of affiliation for their city, and become aware that they belong. This can facilitate increased engagement across all areas which has the potential to boost economic input. As they share these experiences with families, friends, and even business owners, there is the possibility that there will be an uptick of people who move to your city, and that the people who relocate will be more active residents who participate in city offerings. If you are a parent who has a child with autism or are an adult with autism, and you have a choice to move to a city that is Autism Friendly versus one that is not, where would you choose to work and live?

Chapter 3

Listen to Your Community

I want the world to be more accepting.
I want a seat at the table and to feel included in
every part of society.

– Haley Moss

Being an Autism Friendly City helps you open doors to your
community. It shows that you are committed to gaining a
greater understanding of those that you serve. Part of acquir-
ing this knowledge is taking the time to hear the needs of
your residents. People want to feel heard and they want to
contribute their thoughts, ideas, and concerns. This begins
with listening.

Survey Your Residents

It is useful to gather information directly from the people
who live in your town. You may ask about their experiences
interacting with city staff, or how their needs might be better

DOI: 10.4324/9781003185369-4

met by the city. A resident survey is an effective way to gather this data, and it functions as a needs assessment. The sample provided here is specifically designed to ask questions of your neurodiverse residents and their families. It may be completed by the resident themself, or with support. In instances where the person with autism is a child, a family member is able to complete the survey. The most efficient way to conduct this type of survey is utilizing an online platform that sorts and exports the data in ways that are easily understood so that it can be presented with impact. If you decide to create your own survey, I suggest that you are careful about the reading level, and that you limit the number of questions, to reduce survey fatigue. Also consider the way you present the directions to the survey and how you explain the purpose of the survey. Be direct with your communication. A sample survey is offered as the Resident Survey/Needs Assessment. In some instances, a survey may not be the best way to connect with residents, especially if you are responding to a specific incident or situation. In those cases, small group interviews, focus groups, or individual conversations are methods of gathering information that is more personal. Regardless of your approach, be sure to offer the option in multiple languages, and if in-person, at times that are flexible and support a variety of schedules.

*Resident Survey/Needs Assessment

- How long have you lived in the city?

- How frequently do you access city services?

- What type of city services do you utilize?

- If you access services, do you find the directions and information easy to understand?

- What programs and activities do you participate in that are offered by the city?

- If you participate in programs and activities, do you feel welcome?

- During city events or programs, are accommodations that you've requested been provided for you or your child?

- Are you able to successfully and easily navigate the city's website? If not, how can we improve this for you?

- When you communicate with city employees, are you able to easily understand the information they provide? If not, please suggest how we can do this better.

■ Do you believe that city staff have a good understanding of people with autism?

■ Have you had an experience where you felt like you could not access city services or programs? If yes, please provide a description and indicate the barrier to accessibility.

■ What services or supports can the city offer that will improve your experience?

■ Do you find city leadership approachable and responsive?

■ Would you be willing to participate on an Inclusion Team that advises the city on best practices related to being Autism Friendly, or are you willing to provide us with feedback about the city in a one-on-one environment?

■ Would you like to provide your contact information and be added to an email list to receive updates on the Autism Friendly Cities initiative?

What You Might Hear

After conducting a resident survey, it is possible the responses you receive may make you uncomfortable or upset. You may have believed that your city was doing a better job with inclusion than what your residents are actually experiencing. You may discover incidents or situations that you were unaware of. For some situations, you may wish to follow up directly with a resident. When that is not possible, it is helpful to explore what happened and where there was a breakdown in your city. These are areas where your staff is likely to need training.

Many residents are generally satisfied with their city but are not frequently engaged with what is offered, so they may not be able to provide much feedback on city programs. It is equally important to find out more information from those residents about why they do not participate and determine what is needed so they will increase their participation. Perhaps an individual is interested in attending a city festival, but they know they will need to take a break during the day. Designating a quiet space will open up the event to that individual, which is a simple and effective strategy that increases accessibility. However, it is not enough to simply implement a strategy. If your residents are not made aware of what will be available they may continue to not attend events. Utilize the resident survey as an information-gathering tool but also as a way to develop a contact database to share updates with your residents.

People with autism want to experience life. They want to feel like they belong. This is an area where people with autism are sometimes misunderstood. They seek opportunities for social engagement, forums to develop relationships, ways to engage in the community, employment in their own town, and a life with a sense of purpose. Be sure to listen to their needs and acknowledge their experience, utilizing their input to create a neurodiverse community.

Tend Your Garden

Gardens require sun, water, weeding, pruning, planning, and care. While growing your city and adding an initiative, such as being Autism Friendly, it is necessary to continue to tend your garden. Sustain the quality services you offer your residents while you consider the results of your resident survey, and process the feedback. Listen to the needs of your team and your leadership, to help set the groundwork and build a foundation for your initiative to launch from. While working to improve your city and bring new members in, care for the relationships with those who are currently invested in the city, and listen for how they can continue to be cultivated. Add this new initiative with intent and thoughtfulness, weaving it into your community. Tend your garden and your city will thrive.

THE WHO

2

People with Autism, Leaders, and Community Partners

> As human beings, our job in life is to help people realize how rare and valuable each one of us really is, that each of us has something that no one else has - or ever will have - something inside that is unique to all time. It's our job to encourage each other to discover that uniqueness and to provide ways of developing its expression.
>
> **– Fred Rogers**

It is difficult to develop strategies and supports without knowledge, and it is impossible to have a successful initiative in solitude. We can't create change without information, and we definitely cannot do it alone. We absolutely must include the people with autism and neurodiversity. This section will

DOI: 10.4324/9781003185369-5

provide a brief overview of autism, will discuss training opportunities, how to determine what your needs are, and discuss how to connect with trainers in your region. It will also guide you through the process of putting together an Inclusion Team and how to connect with your community organizations. Once that team is in place, it will guide you on how to utilize the experience and expertise of those group members and how to reap the benefit of those collaborations.

Chapter 4

Let's Talk about Autism

I am different, not less. The world needs all types of minds.

– Temple Grandin

They say that when you've met one person with autism, you've met one person with autism. This is absolutely true. While there are some overarching commonalities within neurodiverse communities, and some similar issues that this group faces, every person with autism will have their own abilities, support needs, personality, and goals.

This chapter will contain a general overview of autism. To help you assess your team's learning, a short quiz is provided that can be utilized as a pre-test and/or post-test. We will review basic diagnostic information about autism, the rates and prevalence of autism, the characteristics that some people with autism may present with, difference versus deficit, and neurodiversity. My goal with this chapter is to bridge the understanding of the diagnosis to those who are inexperienced or unfamiliar with the needs and general characteristics of individuals with autism. As such, this chapter will not contain highly academic or medical data, but the foundational information critical to developing an Autism Friendly initiative.

DOI: 10.4324/9781003185369-6

*Quiz (Pre-/Post-test): A Brief Quiz on Autism

1. What is the prevalence of autism according to the US CDC?

     a. 1 in 1,730   b. 1 in 260   c. 1 in 44   d. 1 in 98

2. Is autism an intellectual disability?

     a. Yes   b. No

3. There is a blood test to diagnose autism.

     a. True   b. False

4. Autism is more prevalent in males.

     a. True   b. False

5. What are the three main areas of difference for individuals with autism?

     a. _____   b. _____   c. _____

6. It can be said that behavior is _____

     a. Willful   b. Communication   c. Mental health issue

7. Being different automatically means that a person has a deficit.

     a. True   b. False

Basic Diagnostic Information

Autism is a complex developmental disorder that presents as a spectrum. Autism is not an intellectual disability. This is an important distinction, because there are some people who think autism is related to intelligence. That is not the case. There may be individuals who have both autism and an intellectual disability, but they are different diagnoses. It is important to understand that autism presents on a continuum, where some individuals will exhibit more characteristics and have more support needs than others. Individuals with autism may present with some features, communication challenges, and behaviors, but not others, and may experience a varying intensity of specific parts of autism. While there are overarching distinctions of autism, all people with autism, like everyone in society, are unique.

People with autism may have co-occurring diagnoses where they experience autism and a mental illness or physical disability. It is sometimes possible that the co-occurrence presents more significantly than the autism or vice versa. For example, a person with autism might also have a diagnosis of depression. There may be times in that person's life when their autism is more pronounced and other times when their depression is more prominent.

Autism can be diagnosed at any time in life, but it is most frequent to see the diagnosis during early childhood. A diagnosis often results from a family's interaction with a team of practitioners, which may be in consultation with a psychologist, the child's pediatrician, with a specific service provider, such as a speech and language pathologist, or through an early intervention or school-based team. When considering the diagnostic criteria of autism, it is important to recognize that it is a multifaceted developmental disorder that has no known cause, no current medical tests for the diagnosis (such as a blood test), no ethnic racial or cultural boundaries, and no socioeconomic boundaries. Early diagnosis and intervention, when possible, is the best practice and most supportive of the child's needs throughout early development and early education.

Prevalence

At the time of the writing of this book, the US Center for Disease Control indicates that 1 in 44 individuals is diagnosed with an autism spectrum disorder (2021). The rate of autism in the United Kingdom is 1 in 57 children. From a global perspective, the World Health Organization reports that 1 in 270 people has an autism spectrum disorder. The prevalence of autism continues to rise, as in the United States in the 1980s and 1990s approximately 1 in 2,500 people was diagnosed with autism. Autism is the fastest-growing developmental disability. Autism is more prevalent in males, with the ratio of diagnosis for males to females being approximately 5 to 1. Historically, girls exhibit variations on characteristic aspects of autism, and research supports the likelihood that they are under-represented in the current prevalence rates. There is also research that supports an under-representation of autism in the Hispanic and Black communities, with new efforts to connect and communicate more with those groups, to try and increase early and accurate diagnosis.

Characteristics

The three main aspects of autism are social, communication, and behavioral differences. Other parts of autism are expressed as challenges with executive functioning (which includes planning, organization, and time management), restricted or limited interests, and rigidity around schedules and structure. Autism presents as a spectrum, which means there is a range and varying scope of which areas of living may require more support or may be more prevalent in their presentation for the individual.

People with autism may communicate differently or exhibit behaviors that are distinctive, unique, and possibly unfamiliar to you. They may have varied language or be nonverbal. Some will utilize technology, cards, or signs to converse or indicate a need or want. A person with autism may display poor eye contact, have a monotone voice, perseverate on ideas, and act unexpectedly in ways that might include self-stimulating or soothing behaviors such as spinning, flapping, or picking. They may have a low threshold for sensory stimulation and exhibit what is viewed as a "meltdown" that may be caused by excess stimulation and can become sensory overload, which triggers a behavioral response. An individual may present with echolalia, which is when words, phrases, or questions are repeated, potentially in recurring ways.

It is possible that a person with autism has sensory hypersensitivity or hyposensitivity, which means an individual might be over- or under stimulated by certain sensory experiences. Some sensory experiences that a person with autism might have difficulty with include crowds, loud sounds, small spaces, textures, lighting, certain smells, visual stimuli, touch and tactile sensation, taste, temperature, and unexpected sensory experiences, such as an alarm that may go off without warning. Some examples of how these sensory-related behaviors can manifest are that an individual may only wear clothes that are a specific material and that don't have tags, a haircut can be a challenging tactile experience, they may wear headphones to block out noise, or they may have difficulty eating foods with certain textures.

Individualisms that people with autism may experience include difficulty making friends, a preference for routine and constancy, partiality for predictability, and social challenges that can include things like initiating or ending a conversation. When learning to understand behavior, it is important to recognize that behavior is a method of communication, which means that when a person with autism is demonstrating a behavior, they are communicating a need, want, or response to stimuli. It could be that a person is desiring something tangible or physical and they are reaching for it, or that they may try to escape or avoid a particular situation where they are experiencing too much sensory stimulation. A person may display a certain type of self-soothing behavior that they utilize to aid them feel more comfortable due to stimuli that are beyond their control, which is impacting them in a certain way. Those behaviors will manifest in ways unique to an individual and may or may not be particularly observable.

As a city employee, providing support for behavior is dependent on the situation. For example, if you are working one-on-one with an adult and you observe that they are displaying a behavior, or that the frequency of a behavior has increased (such as clicking the end of a pen cap), it is useful to stop the conversation and ask if there is anything that they are worried or anxious about, or if there is something in the environment that can be changed, like turning off a fan or reworking the lighting. When you are planning an event, having a low-sensory or quiet space available for people who may need a moment apart from a crowd or loud noises can be a behavioral supportive. If you experience a parent who has a child exhibiting a behavior, you can help by asking the parent if there is anything you can do to support them. Recognize that parents often endure a lot of judgment in public when this happens, and helping them in a flexible, open, and nonjudgmental way can be a great relief.

Difference versus Deficit

I'd like to take a moment in this section to discuss the concept of difference versus deficit. In medical terminology, and what has become a societal construct, people with disabilities are frequently seen as those who have a deficit in an area. As human rights have grown and developed, it is important to acknowledge that difference does not mean deficit. Over my many years of working with individuals with autism, especially the teen and young adult population, it is clear to me that we all have a unique way of being, and that does not necessarily prevent any person from reaching their goals and dreams. Our world is neurodiverse, and individuality should be celebrated. I support evidence-based practices and therapies to help both children and adults with autism develop skills to navigate the world as it is. I also believe that as a society, we need to do better to shift the lens of difference.

There is a movement within the autism community right now that is exploring modifying some of the language that is used around their identification. For example, it has always been best practice to use person-first language, which is discussed in the communication section of this book: that an individual is a 'person with autism' instead of an 'autistic person.' However, people with autism are identifying themselves in ways now that puts their autism front and center, without shame or hesitation. It may be that a person with autism will identify themselves to you in a way that is not person first because that is how they are most comfortable. As such, when working with anyone with a disability, it is important to meet them where they are, and to respect their choice and method of identification.

Neurodiversity

A term that has entered the conversation more recently is neurodiversity. In the past, we've considered the concept of diversity from a cultural and ethnic perspective. Neurodiversity describes people who have varying ways of cognitively processing the world around them. Neurodiverse people may or may not have autism. They may be individuals with other types of mental functioning, or different methods of processing. It could be that their intellectual abilities vary or that their communication style is not traditional. It is important that we include neurodiversity as part of the Autism Friendly movement because it expands the breadth and the depth of inclusion.

Hard Conversations

What happens when you feel uncomfortable, or you don't know what to say or do, when you encounter a person with autism? Please understand that it is okay to have those feelings. These types of concerns have been brought to my attention many times while facilitating a training about autism. Or, more often, I've had someone pull me aside after a training to privately to ask this kind of question, because they might feel a little ashamed.

The most important things to remember when you feel uncomfortable is to not to rush to judgment, and to ask questions. For example, when you encounter somebody who communicates differently than you, it may be frustrating or challenging to understand their needs, especially when you are trying to help. What you can do is ask questions that aid your understanding. Ask the person about their communication methods, or try to communicate using a different technique yourself. Be patient while they express themselves.

Even if you get flustered, remain calm and take a moment to step into that person's shoes. They are trying to communicate and are also becoming discouraged because they are being misunderstood. If you find that you are in over your head, ask the person if they have anyone available to help you understand their needs, or you may possible have a colleague that has more experience working with people with autism that can help.

*Pre-/Post-test Quiz Answers

1. C

2. B

3. B

4. A

5. a. Social   b. Communication   c. Behavior

6. B

7. B

Chapter 5

Training

Until we create a nation that regularly wants to employ a person with autism, assure for a quality education for each person with autism, and eliminates the far too many unnecessary obstacles placed in the way of success for a person with autism, we really won't be as successful as we must. We need to get all in our nation to embrace the belief that each person with autism is valued, respected and held to the highest level of dignity and must be provided every opportunity for the highest quality of life each and every day.

**– Scott Badesch, Autism Society
of America Past-President**

Information is power. The chapter on autism provided in this book may not offer enough detailed information for certain city staff, as it is designed to be a brief overview. More in-depth training is especially important for first responders, law enforcement, recreation staff, and camp counselors who will have unique and more individualized contact with people with autism. This chapter will guide the reader on what to

DOI: 10.4324/9781003185369-7

look for in a both a general training provider and one that can match the more comprehensive needs of your city. It will also review how to obtain training, ways to deliver it to your staff, and what is needed after the initial training to continue the conversation.

What Training Does My Team Need?

When considering training needs, realize that there are two types of city staff. There are those who are resident-facing (meaning they interact directly with members of your community), and those who are not. For employees who are not resident-facing, a basic overview of autism is useful to ensure they are included in the Autism Friendly initiative. While they may not work with the public, they will certainly have colleagues, and it is possible that those colleagues could be on the autism spectrum. For staff who work directly with residents, a more in-depth training is needed. How in-depth, depends on the role of the staff member. A person who works the front desk at City Hall is likely to encounter many people with autism and related disabilities, but is not likely to work very closely with them over a long period of time. An employee in the role of a teacher or coordinator, who is providing a direct program, such as an arts and crafts specialist, or a basketball coach, is more likely to have sustained direct interactive contact with a person with autism. Those team members would definitely benefit from an overview, but they will also require a secondary or more expansive training that includes strategies on how to work closely with the resident they are serving in specific situations. When consulting with a trainer or educational organization, it will be important to share with them the roles of the staff being trained, as well as any concerns or potential issues that may have come up in the past that need to be addressed. This way the facilitator can be prepared to provide the level of information that is needed and to address and individualize the training for the needs of your city.

If you are feeling apprehensive about engaging an educator for this initiative, or are not sure exactly what level of training your staff needs, I've provided guidance in the form of a questionnaire to help with the process. You will want to begin with a foundational autism overview, and from there you can conduct a brief survey of your employees and ask them what they believe their needs are, as well as their gaps of knowledge in this area. When initially seeking a trainer, look in your local community to determine if there is an autism-related agency that can meet your needs that will also have a knowledge and understanding of your region and the residents you serve. You are looking for a person who has education in the area of Special Education, Behavior, Social Work, Disability Studies, or other related autism-related services work. They might also be a Board Certified Behavior Analyst. The facilitator should have direct experience, over several years, of working with individuals with autism. Their background should also include previous delivery of these types of workshops to audiences with similar roles as your city staff, such as recreation specialists.

*Worksheet: Questions for Potential Trainers

- What is your expertise in the area of autism and related disabilities?

- What is your educational background?

- Are you certified or licensed in an area related to autism or disabilities?

- Describe your experience providing training about autism to city teams.

- Will a person with autism be present for the training or contribute to the development of the training?

- What is the topic and the title of the training?

- Is the training in-person or online?

- How long is the training?

■ How many people from your team will be providing the training?

■ Is there a limit on the size of the audience for a training?

■ Is there a cost for the training?

■ If my team requires a more in-depth training or a follow-up training, is that something you or your organization is able to provide?

■ Is there any technology or materials that we would need to provide as part of the training?

■ What is your availability? Are you able to train our team before or after typical work hours? Or possibly during their lunch break as a lunch and learn?

■ Is there anything we need to do to prepare our team for your training?

■ What training materials will you provide to our team?

How to Continue the Conversation

A one-hour autism overview training is not the end-all and be-all of the education portion of becoming an Autism Friendly City. It is necessary to continue the process of educating staff and supporting their needs as the city adds programs, expands services, or experiences change. It is also important to be sure that new staff receive Autism Friendly training during the onboarding process. Many cities will incorporate an inclusion and/or disability aspect to their new hire orientation and either bring in professionals to offer that training or be trained themselves in a train-the-trainer model. Some facilitators you work with may allow you to record a training, which should include a post-test if viewed as a video outside of a classroom environment.

As staff interact more with people with autism, you may consider encouraging them to make note of things that they need further training on. For example, if a sports coach is working with a child who exhibits some behaviors during a practice, that coach may want to indicate to the inclusion lead that they need a training on behavioral strategies. Other times, planning for continuous training is useful for programs that cycle through staff. For example, summer camp counselors tend to be hired on an annual basis and the new team will need training each year. You may also have program specialists who come to your city to provide just one service. An example might be an artist who is teaching a specific painting class. This person would not be someone who is full-time city staff and likely would not have received this training because they did not attend a new hire orientation. It is helpful to incorporate at least the basics of these workshops into the hiring process even for the very part-time workers or consultants. A training calendar and strategy can be developed by either the inclusion lead, the ADA specialist at your city, or your human resources department.

Chapter 6

Developing Your Inclusion Team: Community Partners Are Key

Alone we can do so little; together we can do so much.

– Helen Keller

One of the most valuable ways to increase inclusionary practice in your city is to bring together your local experts and let them guide you. Developing an Inclusion Team will surround you by people who are equally committed to your initiative and who will be partners to help reach your goal. Not only will this group become an advisory support for your city, but this is also an excellent way to develop relationships with community agencies that work with people with autism. This chapter will review who to include on your team, what types of organizations will be helpful to consult with, how to bring those people together, a sample meeting agenda, and the best way to utilize their expertise to inform your city.

DOI: 10.4324/9781003185369-8

Develop Your Inclusion Team

The process of developing an Inclusion Team typically begins with your city's disability coordinator, outreach specialist, or human resource specialist who is taking the lead on Autism Friendly initiative. Their first step is to reach out to a local autism or disability service agency, service provider, or non-profit organization. To locate this type of group, the internet can be useful, or consider contacting your local school and speaking with the Special Education coordinator.

Directly contacting each individual entity can be time-consuming. A more efficient way to begin exploring the potential support that is available in your region is to seek out an established work group, task force, or committee, where these organizations regularly meet together. Many agencies and nonprofits are already part of community committees, and it is likely that if you can locate one of these groups, you may have access to multiple professionals who can assist you. For example, in my region there is a Special Needs Advisory Council, an Interagency Coalition, and a Transition Task Force, among others. These types of committees may give you the opportunity to present your ideas and describe your needs to a larger number of agencies that can then determine if they have the time and resources to participate. If you'd like to have a one-on-one in-depth conversation before contacting to a larger work group, then I suggest you reach out directly to a single organization that best aligns with your mission, and meet together to brainstorm a partnership and learn about what already exists in your community. As you connect with others, it is useful to create a list of people, agencies, orga-nizations, and nonprofits that exist in your city, that you can develop community partnerships with. From there, hopefully, you will establish relationships across the disability community that can continue to help you broaden your scope.

When meeting professionals that might be interested in being on your Inclusion Team, keep in mind that you will need a variety of perspectives that support and represent the different aspects of what you are trying to accomplish. People will have variety of motivations for signing onto your project, but all of those reasons are important. Find out the "why" at the outset, which might range from an organizational mission of building infrastructure in the community to meeting grant deliverables that require task force participation. Most professionals will participate as part of their job responsibilities, which may require you to consider any conflicts of interests. The teams I have participated on included representatives from organizations that work with people with autism, developmental disabilities, intellectual disabilities, people who are blind, deaf, dyslexic, or have cerebral palsy, among others. You want to be sure to include people with autism, at least one parent, an educator, and organizational representatives that have the professional expertise, which encompasses direct service. Be sure to also consider gender, culture, age, socioeconomic factors, and of course neurodiversity.

Titles for your Inclusion Team can be straightforward or creative and may change as the purpose of the group becomes clear and the goals develop. For example, I've known groups to be called the following: Inclusion Support Team, ADA Consulting Group, Inclusion Consulting Team, Special Needs Work Group, or Special Needs Advisory Team. A good approach is to invite the potential participants to the table and let them work together during the first meeting to name the team.

Depending on your city structure, it will be prudent to work with your community leaders, who could be politicians. A city leader might want to participate on your Inclusion Team, or receive regular updates. You may discover that you need to present your initiative for approval and be prepared to explain the return on investment and potential use of city resources. Education will also be needed to help your leaders with understanding and learning more about people with autism. There are many leaders who support these types of inclusionary initiatives but may not be willing to spend the time or money needed to do it well. If you find that this is the case, it may be useful to connect with a city that has become Autism Friendly and share their model and success with your leadership team.

Brainstorm and utilize the worksheet: Create Your Inclusion Team. Consider who might be useful from both inside and outside of your city. It is important to include at least one individual with autism on your Inclusion Team, as well as a parent, both of whom would ideally be representative of the people who participate in your programs.

*Worksheet: Create Your Inclusion Team

Potential City Staff Team Members

Name	Department	Job Title	Reason to Include	Contact Information
Cornelius Pool	Parks and Rec	Swim Program Director	Share needs of swim program	c.pool@city.org

Potential Community-Based Team Members

Name	Organization	Job Title	Reason to Include	Contact Information
Leonard Specialist	Autism Center	Clinician	Provide autism expertise	Leonard@ asdctr.org

Location and Timeframe for Meetings

Most Inclusion Teams will either meet quarterly or once a month. Monthly is typically best, as cities usually have many projects and programs occurring throughout the year. It is important to recognize that the people on your team may have certain seasons that are busier for them or times they are not in the office, such as teachers or educators who have summer break. When designing your meeting structure and calendar, be sure to consider location. Some Inclusion Teams will always meet in the same conference room in the city that they are supporting. Other teams will rotate the specific location around the city so they have the opportunity to tour and view various buildings and city spaces. Some teams will meet at their members' offices or programs so that they have the opportunity to learn about the local services being offered and to deepen those relationships. Throughout COVID-19, many groups met online, which allowed for more attendees, but not for the knowledge and community-building that comes with in-person experiences.

A good timeframe for meetings is approximately an hour and a half. One hour tends to be a bit short, and two hours can be a long time for people to hold focus. There may be opportunities to extend a meeting if the group is also touring a facility or program as part of the gathering. Other reasons to lengthen a meeting is if your larger team has small work groups that require time to convene and discuss a specialty area, project, or an event they are planning. Options for additional meetings can include inviting your members to train the group about their organization or population, or to include the team in city planning meetings where they can provide expertise and contribute.

Inclusion Team Meeting Agenda

During your first Inclusion Team meeting it is essential to orient the team to your city and each other. When designing a meeting agenda for your Inclusion Team, it is important to include time at the beginning for introductions and what we call 'agency updates'. This is an opportunity for each team member to be able to share any events, programs, or changes going at their organization. Perhaps it is a disability awareness month, or possibly there is a fundraiser or conference being offered by one of the representatives. Your meeting can be a forum for these professionals to share information with each other and see where there may be some overlap or opportunities for partnerships. This is also an important time for your city representative to hear what's going on in the local community and to listen for where they might be able to plug in or support each other. Perhaps an agency is having an outreach event where they are providing tables for different groups to share their materials. Your city, for example, might want to bring some of your program staff to the event where they can offer information, and begin to really connect with and invite members of the disability community. In some instances, a city may even collaborate on an event to benefit both the residents and the organizations on the Inclusion Team.

One of the most important parts of the Inclusion Team is to provide input and feedback on upcoming city events, projects, and inclusion strategies for the city. This is going to be the core of the meeting and where the expertise of this group will be guiding the city. It is useful for the city to provide an update of where they are on their autism-specific or disability-specific projects. For example, you may be creating a social story related to a child's first time attending a summer camp at your city. It is useful to share these things with the group so they can provide feedback and suggestions. The city may a be hosting an event during which the Inclusion Team representatives can participate and share their disability service-related information with residents of that city.

Outside of regular Inclusion Team meetings, it may be prudent to invite members of the committee to provide expertise on specific projects. For example, when the City of Boynton Beach was designing its downtown remodeling project, I was invited in several times to speak with the architects and city planners about safety concerns. These discussions included ways to incorporate visual and physical barriers to increase safety. Things like wayfinding and low sensory spaces were also discussed. When remodeling existing spaces, or creating new one, bring in your Inclusion Team to provide input.

Sample Inclusion Team Meeting Agenda

INCLUSION TEAM MEETING AGENDA
Date
Location

I.   Introductions

II. Agency/Organization Updates and Upcoming Events

III. City General Update

IV. Proclomations or Celebrations

V.   City Projects That Could Benefit From Team Input

VI. Review of Previous Projects/Follow-Up

VII. Fundraising/Sponsorship/Any Financial Reviews

VIII. Team or Project Goals

IX. Collaborative Event Planning

X.   Proposed Next Meeting Date, Time, And Location

* Capture attendance and update contact information during sign-in.

Team Collaborations and Projects

Outside of regular meetings, and reviewing your schedule of events with the Inclusion Team, there are other ways to expand your partnerships and to develop further collaborations. It is likely that members of your team may bring ideas that are founded in their knowledge of autism or their disability area, and may request to provide training for your city staff. This training can be in different specialty areas. For example, someone who works with the deaf population may be interested in training your first responders in some basic sign language and communication techniques. Other collaborations might include options for having the city participate in or sponsor an organization's service program. For example, an agency that provides behavioral therapy for children might be interested in a day when the police department brings out their canine unit and the therapist works on animal familiarity with a particular child or group of children.

One example of a partnership was at the City of Boynton Beach, where they utilized their Inclusion Team connections to collaborate with a middle school and create a program for Arbor Day. The city park manager and a teacher created a project for students and city staff to plant trees. This was very successful in bringing together students with disabilities and the parks department in the city. Another example is a multi-year collaboration I was directly involved with, an Art and Autism Expo at the City of Boynton Beach. These expos brought together artists who were autistic with the team at the city's Cultural Center. For one event, the artists were able to display their art throughout the center's public spaces wing, and were the official Art in Public Places group for the summer. That event culminated in a Breaking Barriers reception and an opportunity for the artists to sell their work. Another Art and Autism Expo was held during COVID-19 times and was a hybrid event where artists were able to showcase their art around the city and provide videos of the art being created or explained, to be highlighted in an online program. These expos provided incredible opportunities for the artists as they were celebrated and shared their talents. It was also extremely beneficial for the city, as their Art in Public Places program was able to expand inclusion by connecting people with autism and bringing their creativity into city spaces. A poster from one of the City of Boynton Beach Art in Public Places programs is shown here.

Regional or State-wide Inclusion Teams

Once your Inclusion Team is established, there might be an opportunity to expand the team outside of your city. Some teams might grow into large work groups that include multiple cities or entire counties. When this occurs, it can be beneficial because there is an opportunity to share ideas and to collaborate on larger projects. While this type of larger regional team can be useful, it is recommended to also continue to have your own city's Inclusion Team meetings to continually provide support for your projects, events, and programs.

THE WHAT

Creating Change

3

Every great dream begins with a dreamer. Always remember, you have within you the strength, the patience, and the passion to reach for the stars to change the world.

– Harriet Tubman

The passion and motivation of a single person is often at the inception of a grassroots movement. If you are the one who is reading this book, then it is straightforward: creating change is up to you. It is your job to start the process.

Change can be difficult. While leading the transformation of a city and the 'what' that needs to be done, it is important to remember to frame it in the 'why.' When Simon Sinek talks about his golden circle and that organizations need to start with their 'why,' he is explaining that teams, and in this case, your city, needs to revisit their cause and their purpose. As a society we tend to be very outcome driven, but to truly make systemic alterations, we must look at our reasons why and

DOI: 10.4324/9781003185369-9

begin there. If it is your city's core mission to serve all the residents that live in your community, then removing barriers, increasing access, and celebrating neurodiversity are going to be at the heart of your 'why.'

Chapter 7

Getting Started

Our ability to reach unity in diversity will be the
beauty and the test of our civilization.

– Mahatma Gandhi

What is inclusion? Inclusion is not simply acceptance, it
is a concept that goes well beyond just knowing about or
acknowledging differences, but celebrating that diversity and
recognizing what makes each one of us unique. It is in that
distinctiveness that people come together to create community.
Strong societies include many ways of being. We can focus
on commonalities to help bring us together, but also seek to
discover and understand our individuality to ensure that all
people are able and encouraged to participate.

DOI: 10.4324/9781003185369-10

In my experience working with cities, there are some that express interest in being Autism Friendly but that are not fully ready to engage with the entire process. This tends to be the case especially with larger cities that feel overwhelmed at the idea of training thousands of staff and developing the strategies required to accompany the implementation. One way to help navigate interest without large-scale commitment is to encourage pick one group or department to engage with the process. That would mean training those staff, interacting with community agencies for consultation, and then implementing a few strategies for improved access. For example, this might look like creating an Autism Friendly swimming department. The swim teachers and coaches, along with the lifeguards at the pool, are trained about autism. Visual supports are created for the physical space, and a social story is developed for individuals who are new to using the pool or first-time swimmers. The consultation for the department may be a quarterly meeting with a local autism expert who provides suggestions on working one-on-one with children who might exhibit behaviors. In this case, it would not be that the entire city that is designated as Autism Friendly but that there is an Autism Friendly swimming pool or swimming program within the city. What frequently occurs is once there is a unit within a city that has completed these first steps, other groups and departments can see what kind of time and resources were required and be motivated to participate. They may also use the department as a success story or a model within the city to expand inclusion efforts. Conversations about starting the process can be forwarded by utilizing the worksheet here.

*Worksheet: What Does Inclusion Look Like for Your City?

Share five words that describe inclusion:

1.

2.

3.

4.

5.

What is special about your town or city that you will need to be aware of when creating an neurodiverse community?

What barriers to inclusion do you anticipate?

What programs and initiatives have you already created that improve access?

In a perfect world, with no financial obstacles, and unlimited resources, what would your ideal neurodiverse community look like for your city?

Chapter 8

Environmental Modifications and Sensory Consideration

This chapter will explore the physical spaces in your city and how small modifications can be made to improve accessibility. Locations include physical space in city buildings, outside areas, safety across your city, creating low-sensory spaces, and developing environmental accessibility strategies. When we design sensory-friendly spaces, we want to consider our senses and how they react to stimuli. Traditionally there are five senses, but we are going to expand that a bit and discuss those that might be an issue for a person with autism.

Sight

Our eyes give us information about in the visual aspects of our surroundings. They also are receptors of light. For people with autism, they may experience sensitivity to certain types of visual stimuli, different kinds of lighting and levels of

DOI: 10.4324/9781003185369-11

lighting. Visual stimuli might present as certain colors, combinations of colors, or patterns. Many colors or images together at once might elicit a feeling of overwhelm. These types of visual stimuli can appear anywhere, from websites to walls, and flyers to sign-up forms. Be aware of color choices, the number of items or questions you place on a page, spacing, and how you choose to organize information.

Lighting, especially high-intensity UV lights from above, also can cause a person to have a behavioral or emotional reaction. Lighting that can be modified is useful and can support a more welcoming environment. For example, using lamps in small spaces instead of UV lights and having dimmable lights can be much better options. For outdoor activities, consider offering sun glasses as a giveaway or inform participants if shade is not available.

Hearing

The ears interpret sound waves. People with autism may be sensitive to sound. They may experience anxiety or a behavior change if a sound is interpreted as too loud for them. Noise also comes in the form of ambient sound, which are the background sounds that we may not typically focus on, but that are in the environment. These types of noises can include the hum of air conditioners or lights, possibly background music or people talking nearby, or other machinery like an elevator motor. When creating environments, it is important to consider how much sound we are pumping into the background. I encourage you to sit quietly in your space for five minutes and listen for the ambient sounds that you may typically not focus on because you filter it out. A person with autism might have a more difficult time not hearing those noises and may be unable to separate it from direct sound. As such, you may see people with autism wearing headphones or earplugs in order to help them modify sound level so that it works best for their own quality of life. When designing city space, consider materials that may decrease echo and reduce ambient sound. If you are choosing a location for a quiet area or low-sensory room, it is important to consider what is nearby and how sound may impact that space.

Touch

Individuals with autism may experience sensitivity to touch. This may be increased when the person initiating touch is unfamiliar to them. For example, if a recruiter offers a hand for a handshake at the beginning of an interview, it may be challenging for the applicant to shake the hand, or they might refuse. It is important that this is not interpreted as a sign of rejection and that it is not taken personally. An approach to this type of situation is to ask a person if they'd like to shake hands and to be nonjudgmental and supportive if they decline.

There are individuals with autism who will have touch sensitivity related to clothing. They may be most comfortable clothes made out of certain fabric, like cotton and require that the tags be removed. This can be challenging if the city is offering a sports program where wearing a particular uniform is mandatory, and not complying means you are not able to participate. An easy way to improve access in that situation is to work with clothing companies that design tag-free clothes in a variety of fabrics. Many main stream stores are now offering sensory-friendly clothing lines.

Smell

Smells can permeate a space very easily. From cleaning supplies to odors that come from the staff kitchen, smells are everywhere. When ordering supplies to clean with, it can be helpful to go with neutral scents or use chemicals that are fragrance free. This is especially important if the city is offering things like towels at a swimming pool, which get washed in industrial laundry detergent. For programs where people come together in small spaces, it can be useful to request that people do not wear strong perfumes or body sprays in order to help keep the environment as fragrance free as possible. When cooking in a group, consider either eating outdoors, away from strong smells, or having the entire event in a well-ventilated or open-air setting.

Taste

It is likely that a city may offer food items during a celebration, an event, or a child's program or camp. In these situations, it is useful to offer foods that have varying tastes and textures. For example, if tacos are being offered, having an option for a soft taco and a hard taco would give an individual a choice for texture. When working one-on-one in a food-related setting, the best option is to consult with the individual or family beforehand to determine likes and dislikes, and, when possible, offer choices.

Temperature

Temperature can be a concern for a person with autism. For some, they may feel uncomfortable experiencing sweat on their bodies. Others may have physical response to extreme cold. When having outdoor events, it is important to incorporate temperature regulation into the quiet space or sensory-friendly space. For example, if your event is outdoors in a hot climate, it can be useful to have your quiet space in a nearby air-conditioned building, or at least in a shaded area. In colder climates, having warming options such as outdoor heaters or blankets can be useful. If you are hosting an activity in a room that typically gets cool, suggest on the flyer, that participants bring a sweater or jacket with them.

Spatial

There are some individuals with autism who have challenges with spatial relations. This may mean that they have a difficult time judging distance and direction. They may also have trouble with navigation. Utilizing visual supports that mark sides of a path, providing clear step-by-step direction, and creating maps and wayfinding strategies that incorporate visual supports, can be helpful.

High and Low-Sensory Spaces

When designing spaces, we may often hear about a sensory-friendly space. What we are usually not told, is if the designation is meaning a low-sensory space or a high sensory space. It is important to differentiate between the two, both for yourself as you engage with the design process and for your families. If a child is overstimulated in a program or event, and they enter a sensory-friendly zone in order to have a break from the stimuli, and they walk into a room full of high sensory objects, it may be quite detrimental for them.

When creating a low-sensory space, we want to consider what's discussed above and offer a calm place with low lighting, minimal to no sound, soft furniture, and walls with little to no distraction. When creating a high sensory space, we may incorporate bolder colors, tactile experiences, ways to move the body, or activities that engage motor skills.

*Worksheet: Design Your Space

Explore a space you are considering modifying. This worksheet will guide you through the experience.

- ■ What is the purpose of the space you are creating?

- ■ Who is this space for? (Children, teens, adults, families?)

- ■ Is the goal of the space to be high sensory or low sensory?

- ■ How will the space serve your residents? When are they most likely to use it?

- ■ What items do you currently have that can be used or modified? (i.e., furniture, lighting)

- ■ What items do you need? (Fidgets, high-tactile boards, blankets, mats)

- ■ Does the space require painting or other environmental changes?

- ■ Is the space easily accessible to those it is intended for? Is it multiuse space?

- ■ Where is the door to the room? Does it lead to a parking lot or water? Can an alarm and visual support be installed on the door?

- ■ What other safety-related modifications are needed? (i.e., does the space have outlet covers? Are heavy items, like a tv, mounted to the wall? Does the furniture move easily?)

Chapter 9

Communication Techniques

This chapter will offer you strategies and suggestions on how to improve your communication approach when working with individuals with autism. These supports will include verbal communication, email, print materials, and marketing.

Communication is how we share ideas and information. When we provide this information to the residents of our communities, they are able to make informed decisions related to how they live, when they engage, and the way in which they are able to access services. When we communicate, we are doing it in many ways: through the internet, newsletters, text alerts, flyers, brochures, phone calls; and billboards. Utilizing an Autism Friendly approach can help us be sure that the information we share it is received and understood.

It is important to start off by helping to make people feel welcome. Everyone wants to feel welcome. Offer an open-door policy for communication by having public meetings, suggestion boxes, and availability. When that isn't possible, provide office hours, or frequent meetings by appointment to help your residents feel that they have opportunities to be heard.

Direct Communication

When I teach organizations about being Autism Friendly and we discuss communication, I challenge them to go an entire day without using a simile, metaphor, or cliché and to only use direct communication. This is more difficult than most people believe. We frequently use words and phrases that have multiple meanings. For example, when we say "It's raining cats and dogs" we don't mean that animals are falling from the sky, and when we say "Every cloud has a silver lining," we don't mean that the clouds have metallic interiors. When we speak in those ways, we can easily be confusing. For someone who is on the autism spectrum, it may be difficult for them to understand what we actually mean when we use these types of phrases. Unfortunately, this can lead to a person misinterpreting what you were trying to tell them, and if you were attempting to communicate directions, the result can be that the individual does not have the information to follow through on something important. There are times when this can be particularly detrimental to a person's life. I have observed professionals see the confusion in the eyes of an individual they are working with, and instead of rewording what they are trying to explain using direct communication, they repeat the same phrase multiple times. Occasionally, they even begin to raise their voice. This is not helpful. If you have an experience where it is apparent that you are being misunderstood, try to use alternate words that are logical, clear, and direct. Rephrase with words that have singular meaning.

When you work directly with a resident, offer information that can prevent miscommunication in the future. Be straightforward about your office hours and availability. Discuss the roles and responsibilities of your city, and ways your city is able to help. Set expectations plainly and early on in the interaction. It can be useful to answer the following questions and provide the answers as a guide to residents you work with:

- Do you allow walk-in appointments?
- What is your typical timeframe to return voice messages? (24 hrs?)
- What is your preferred method of communication? (phone, email)
- Explain what you consider urgent and what is not urgent.

Recognize that it will take time to build trust with the individuals you are assisting. Some areas for you to be aware of are:

- Mutual respect
- Reliability
- Resident-centered
- Strong listening skills
- Validate experiences
- Be honest and genuine
- Offering a safe space where a person feels free to share without judgment

One-on-One Communication

One-on-one communication with a resident typically begins when you receive an email, a letter, a phone message, or an in-person walk-in. Let's explore receiving contact via email. The email is likely to be sent to your city's general email box. In the United States, this might be an 'information@yourcity. org' type of email address. It is important to note who is checking your general information email. For some cities this may be done by volunteers, part-time employees, or people who are not in administrative or leadership roles. When you are training your staff, it is important to make sure that these people are included, because they are often the first point of direct contact. When you receive an email from a resident who asks maybe one or two questions. The email may request directions to an event, or for information about how to register for a program, or the time of the next public meeting. Let's use the example of a person who is asking for directions to an event. When responding to an email like this, we may instinctually send a large paragraph of directions that has few spaces and no numbering, which can be overwhelming to a person with autism to decipher. There are some simple steps to make this email more understandable, accessible, and useable. I suggest that you start by breaking the directions down into a bulleted list. After separating out the directions into these smaller statements, and visually organizing them so they each have their own lines, consider choosing either bullets with sequential numbers or bullets that are open circles. The numbered list can be useful because it provides some chronology. For example, it indicates what comes first and what comes next simply by using a set of numbers. The open circles transform the list to a checklist, which allows somebody to either print the list and then check off each direction as they complete it, or to check the boxes off on their phone or computer as they follow each line. While these ideas may appear to be quite simple, the difference for the user, the person who is going to be following these directions, can be significant. When items or tasks are broken down into smaller steps, and they can be marked as complete when the person accomplishes them, it can make an experience that might be overwhelming, into one that is manageable.

One-on-one communication can also help you hear the needs of your residents and identify gaps at your city. For example, if you receive ten phone calls a day from residents asking when the swimming pool will be open, it is advisable to post those hours on your website or in the city spaces. When working closely with residents, consider how you communicate. Using person-first language is a respectful way to address people with disabilities. In this way of communicating, the person always comes first, and not the disability. For example, we want to say that a person is a resident with autism versus an autistic resident. This approach has been the gold standard for many years. However, there are now many individuals with autism who are identifying themselves as autistic people, and may encourage you to not use person-first language with them. Be sure to listen for how the individual you are working with identifies, as this is an ongoing area of change for the community.

An approach to supporting one-on-one communication in meeting settings with residents is to create an agenda template, which can function as a guide when a resident meets with you. This is a document you would provide to your resident and that they can fill out before a meeting, or during a meeting, to help prepare for a subsequent meeting. This is useful because it shows that you support taking notes during a discussion, and that you encourage preparation. There are reminders to help the person bring what is needed to the meeting, as well as prompts to clarify the goal of the meeting.

*Resident Meeting Agenda Template

My Meeting Agenda

Meeting date: _____   Meeting time: _____

Meeting location: _____

Purpose of the meeting: _____

What I need to bring with me to the meeting:

_____

Questions I have for the meeting:

_____

Items or information I need to obtain:

_____

Date, time, and location of the next meeting: _____

_____

Meeting notes:

_____

_____

_____

_____

First Point of Contact

The first point of contact that a resident has with your city has the potential to make or break that resident's relationship with your city. A first point of contact can be many things. It might be when a resident views your website, your listens to the city's recorded phone message, reads a flyer about the city sign on a bulletin board, or speaks to the person sitting behind the front desk at city hall. Each one of these contact points needs to be considered when working through the Autism Friendly process. Is your website clear, consistent, and easy to read? Does it follow the rules of universal design? Do all of your city's flyer have an organized presentation, without too much distraction, and with sufficient visual supports? Was the person who sits at the front desk included in the autism overview training? You may have more touchpoints with your residents than you realize, but each one of them must be reviewed and possibly redesigned to be accessible to everyone.

Universal Design and Websites

In all forms of communication, we want to incorporate aspects of universal design. This approach will allow individuals who use a variety of methods of communication to access and understand what is being shared. Many websites include some features of universal design, while others are fully universal. Accessibility starts with the health and safety of your viewers, which can be eliminating flashes, removing blinking signage or icons, reducing the amount of colors, and adjusting brightness to be easier for the eyes. To enhance the screen view, your resident should be able to adjust the text size, graphic dimension, screen direction; adjustments for a light or dark background; and possibly even change the font type. Fonts are recommended to be simple and without excess ornamentation. Consider spacing, alignment, hyperlink indicators, and animation. The design also includes considering the reading level of your viewer and multiple language accessibility. Some people with disabilities will utilize technology in the form of a screen reader that speaks the text on the screen aloud to them. Make sure that your website can be accessed by these readers and other assistive technology as it progresses.

The next step is to evaluate how the environment of your website looks. Is it flashy, or busy? Is your website full of distractions? Is it difficult to locate items or areas that people might need information about? Are things hidden in drop-down boxes or under a series of lines or characters in corners that require multiple clicks to navigate? Is your website all text? Does it require a high level of literacy? Have you included any visual supports on your website? Do you have icons or graphics that represent areas to visit on your site? For example, if you have regular meetings that are open to the public when you share the calendar of meetings, is there an icon that represents a calendar? If you have a community pool, is there a graphic that shows waves, or a person swimming, which can help make it easily identifiable? Are your icons able to be clicked on for the ease of navigation? The images here show some examples of poor website designs that are complex, are very difficult to understand, and have information hidden. These sites are busy and full of distractions that are likely to give anybody a challenge, but for a person with autism, who may have difficulty with the overstimulation through their senses, they are likely to have a poor experience with this type of website and will move on without obtaining the information they were seeking.

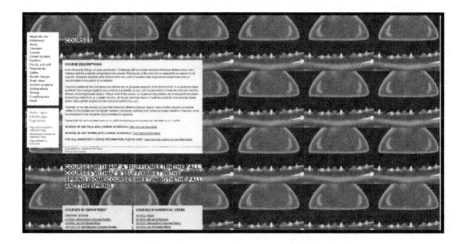

The images below show examples of icon use and mapping.

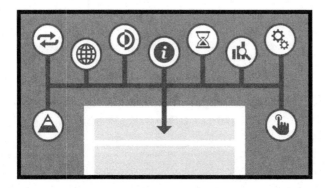

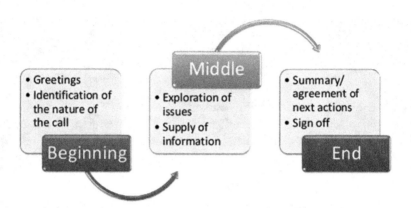

Chapter 10

Visual Supports

This chapter will explain and describe visual supports. It will review their origin and effectiveness. Samples will be included for multiple types of situations and settings.

When I conduct Autism Friendly trainings in person, I am usually accompanied by a cup of caffeine-infused deliciousness from one of the world's most famous coffee houses. I am a huge supporter of their company as I frequent their establishments daily, but I do also use them as an example of how important visual supports can be: Take a moment and imagine that you are a young adult with autism going into one of these coffee cafes for the first time after receiving your first pay check. You are excited to be able to order a blended beverage with whip cream and chocolate drizzle on top. You would like to walk away with the largest size of these beverages that is available. You step into the store and hear the noise of the blender, the sound of people chatting with each other, there is a display case full of delicious snacks, and you see stacks and stacks of cups. The person behind the register asks what size drink you'd like, and when you hesitate for a moment, they tell you the names of the three sizes. The barista says: Tall, Grande, and Venti. Logically, you decide to get a tall. There

DOI: 10.4324/9781003185369-13

is no picture of the cups and no indication of which one is which size. After paying and watching coffee magic happening behind the cappuccino machine, you are excited you will about to receive your coffee drink that you are proud to have spent your hard-earned money on. When the barista hands you your blended beverage, you are confused. The cup is tiny. You see other people with larger cups. You ordered a tall. A tall person is usually the largest person in height. You thought that a tall was the largest cup they offered, because of course it would make sense that a tall is tall. However, this is not the case. Why would the tall cup be tiny? You are frustrated and upset. Your excitement is gone. You walk out of the store with your small blended beverage, disheartened, and thinking to yourself that you will never go into that café again.

What would help our coffee buyer? What would prevent this situation from happening? A visual support. A visual support is a very simple way of providing information beyond the use of words. All this coffee company would need to do is to have pictures of the different cups on a board or at the register and have the names of the sizes underneath the cups. A simpler and cost-free way to do this would be to write the name of the size on the actual cup and put each one on the counter as a visual display. Sometimes such a simple act, such an easy modification, provides accommodation and improves the experience and access for a person with autism.

There are a few different types of visual supports. Some visual supports are simply one shape like a stop sign. This indicates to the person to not go further, or to not open a door, or to stop a particular behavior. Other visual supports might be a little more complex. They might have two or three different items on them indicating what something or multiple items are. While other visual supports are incorporated into a larger word-based item, such as a restaurant menu, where the visuals are pictures or icons on each side of the food description. Some visual supports provide simple directions, such as three steps to withdrawing money at the bank, or three steps to prepare for an art project. Visual supports can also come in the form of a task list. This can be done by creating simple directions and using a design so that the person can check off or ask out the direction once it's completed. For example, using open bubbles for a bulleted list creates a place for a person to check off tasks. Visual supports can be easily developed on a computer and printed out, posted, and updated as needed. The templates and examples shown here are examples of different types of visual supports that were created for use in real-life situations.

*Sample Visual Support Template

How to:

3 EASY STEPS

Step 1:

Step 2:

Step 3:

You are finished!

www.Boynton-Beach.org

*Sample Visual Support
Incorporating Directions

I Get Ready to Paint

Step 1: I put on an apron to keep my clothes clean.

Step 2: I sit down on a chair at the painting table.

Step 3: I wait for instructions before I start to paint.

by Lakeshore

I Clean Up after Painting

Step 1: I put my used paint brush into my cup of water.

Step 2: I take my apron off and put it away.

Step 3: I go to the sink and wash my hands.

*Sample Visual Support Where Graphics Are Incorporated into an Existing Document

Café

 2 Hot Dogs $2.99

Toppings Include: Ketchup, Mayo, Relish, Chili or Sauerkraut, Onion, Cheese

 2 Tacos (choice of beef, chicken or pork) $3.49

Toppings Include: Lettuce, Cheese, Sour Cream and Salsa, Tomatoes

 2 Veggie Tacos $2.49

Choose from: Lettuce, Onion, Peppers, Olives, Sour Cream or Cheese, Tomatoes

 Burrito (choice of beef, chicken or pork) $4.99

Toppings Include: Lettuce, Tomato, Black beans, Sour Cream and Salsa, Rice

 Quesadilla with Cheese (choice of beef, chicken or pork) $4.99

Sour Cream and Salsa served on the side

 Grilled Cheese w/Bacon Combo $5.99

(Choice of American, Swiss or Provolone) Served with chips and a drink.

 Wraps (Choice of any Gourmet Hero) $5.99

Italian, Chicken Salad, Tuna Salad, Turkey and Bacon, Veggie, Corned Beef

 Spaghetti and Meatballs $7.99

Served with a small house salad (lettuce, tomato, cucumber, choice of dressing)

Additional Toppings

 Lettuce   Black Olives   Tomatoes

 Cucumbers   Onion   Carrots

 Cherry Pepper   Alfalfa Sprouts   Jalapenos

 Avocado Spread

Chapter 11

Social Stories

Why is it important for a city to create social stories? There are many opportunities to use this communication aid to help improve accessibility for people with autism. Cities might utilize social stories in a recreation setting, at a library, summer camp programs, and even for special events. This chapter will describe what a social story is and provide directions on how to create one, offering a s sample social story for you to use as a guide.

What Is a Social Story?

Social stories were designed by a teacher named Carrol Gray in the early 1990s. They are used to communicate information, reduce anxiety, and help prepare an individual for a new experience or potentially stressful situation. Social stories are highly visual, and utilize first-person language. For example, one may start by saying "I am going to the park today." It is best practice for a social story to be made available before an event to help decrease stress, and in case any practice is needed prior to participating. The family will read the story together, and the child will have a good idea of what the activity is going to entail, including places where there may be rules or potential challenges. If the social story is only being made available in the physical location where the event is occurring, for example, "today we are learning how to float in the pool," designed to be read by the swim coach, then it is possible that it will need to be reviewed several times before engaging in the activity. There are many types of social stories. They range from Hand Washing to My First Time on an Airplane to Visiting the Doctor.

What Must a Social Story Contain?

Social stories need to contain certain components. They include descriptive, directive, perspective, affirmative, cooperative, control, and partial sentences. It is important to emphasize the detail of the experience, the places where the child may find themselves in a certain type of situation, and areas where that child might have a particular feeling or a response to a situation. For example, your social story might include the sentence, "at the park I will need to wait in line to use the slide. This may feel frustrating." Social stories also emphasize rules and policies of a particular place. We can approach this by offering a choice when there is a requirement. In the sample social story, you will see that a child must take off their shoes to access the gym, which is required. They are provided an embowering point of control when they are given the option to wear socks or go barefoot. The reason to include this in the social story is so the child is aware of this rule ahead of time, and if this is a behavior that needs to be practiced at home, it can be reviewed and rehearsed before entering the setting. It is important to end a social story with acknowledgment. This could be that the child tried something new, or that they had a positive experience at that particular activity or program. It is also important to include reassuring statements for a child throughout the social story. For example, if their parent or a peer is allowed to participate with them, then remind them that they are available in case they need help or have a question. It is also useful to state if there is a bathroom, water, or snacks available during the activity, as it can be useful for a child to know this to help reduce anxiety.

How Can I Create a Social Story?

Social stories are easily created on the computer using word processing or presentation software, such as Microsoft Word or PowerPoint. There are paid social story programs as well as free options available on the internet. Websites also provide templates and graphics to easily design stories. For social stories that are more generic and not location bound, such as When I Feel Upset or When I Have a Bad Dream, there are autism organization that post these types of stories that you might be able to utilize. If you are creating your own social story, it is important to have the background as distraction free as possible, and is typically white or a solid color. The text should be in a large simple font and without too many sentences on each page. The story should be a first-person narrative, and the tense should be present or future, depending on when the activity or experience is taking place, and where the story is located. Some people use clipart or other graphics as a visual aspect. However, it is better practice to use pictures from the actual site of the activity or event in order to make it more recognizable when that child or individual arrives. This sample social story can be used as a model and a template.

*Sample Social Story

The Children's Gym

Social story created in collaboration
with your local autism center

I am going to The Children's Gym!
This is a place I can play!

I can bring snacks and a drink from home.

When I arrive at the gym I need to take off my shoes. I can be barefoot or wear my socks.

At the gym I can choose to swing, jump, run, or climb!

There are adults at the gym help me learn how to use the equipment.

My family member can go on
the trampoline with me!

There will be other children playing at the gym,
and when it is noisy I can go to the quiet space.

I might need to be patient and wait my turn
to use the equipment.

When I want to take a break there is a table where I can color or play with toys.

The gym also has a bathroom and a water fountain that I can use.

I had fun at the gym and I am proud of myself because I tried new things!

Chapter 12

Designing Large-Scale Events

Most cities offer a variety of large-scale events. They can range from arts and craft fairs of just a few hundred attendees to large music festivals with upward of 100,000 people attending. While planning for these events, most cities will commonly consider the needs of people with physical disabilities first and foremost. They will incorporate ramps, large size port-a-potties, and preferred parking, but they do not often think about the needs of an individual with autism. There are many aspects to consider when designing events to make them more accessible to people with autism. In addition to typical accommodations made for people with disabilities, such as sign language interpreters, these are the key areas to consider to address the needs individuals with autism when planning an event:

- Location: Site choice is a major decision. This will set the tone for conversation and decisions on what modifications are needed related to the topics below. Most importantly, site location will determine significant safety aspects that

DOI: 10.4324/9781003185369-15

need to be addressed. The site also contributes to conges-
tion, distance to transportation, ability to include a quiet
area, and ease of communication with staff, vendors, and
attendees.

■ Safety: Water hazards are one of the most important
safety concerns for children with autism at an event. Be
sure to erect barriers that prevent children from going
into water. Safeguarding play areas to keep children far
away from vehicles and moving rides is also necessary. A
child with autism may not abide by signs that indicate not
to go into certain areas, and physical barriers should be
installed when the potential risk is high.

■ Staff knowledge and communication: Consider training
volunteers with an autism overview. This can help them
frame their job duties while considering the needs of neurodiverse attendees.

■ Marketing: When marketing an event, utilize accessibility visuals and icons. This can help attendees know what
supports are available. Including other visual supports or
a social story when sharing event information can also be
useful.

■ Way-finding and maps: When designing way-finding for
an event, either through maps or with apps and digital
technology, be sure to utilize visuals as part of the map.
Visuals include symbols and icons that might indicate
where a low-sensory space is located, as well as identifying potential safety hazards.

■ Signage: Most events will have extensive signage to help
attendees know where to locate things like concessions
or bathrooms. Consider making signs highly visual with
minimal language. Also, having continuity with colors
can be considered a visual support. For example, the sign
indicating the location of the bathroom is green and it is
also green on the map.

■ Quiet or low-sensory spaces: Quiet spaces at events can increase accessibility because an individual with autism may not be willing to attend if there isn't a place available to take a break away from the crowd and the stimulation. A quiet space should be located in an easily reached area, but be at a far enough distance from the crowds to offer some space and serenity.

■ Lost-child area: Large events means that there are chances for children and parents to inadvertently become separated from each other. Indicating a specific safe place where children can either go or be taken to, should they get lost, is useful. This area should be staffed by workers who have at least some basic autism training, and signage should be clear at the location, and on maps of the event.

Chapter 13

An Example: Libraries

Most cities have a library or a library system incorporated into their community. Many libraries fall under the management of a city, and the staff are likely to be city employees. Because of this, I want to share a few ways that libraries can be an inclusive and Autism Friendly place. This chapter will review physical space in a library, opportunities for sensory-friendly browsing, neurodiverse perspectives, and Autism Friendly events. Several of the libraries I've worked with have a special needs department or inclusion specialist as part of their staff. Typically, this specialist is a librarian or children's librarian who has received some extra training or has a degree in this area. Other libraries that may have larger systems in place may have special needs, disability, or inclusion committees or work groups where librarians and staff from across the region or county will gather to develop programs and discuss the needs of their neurodiverse readers.

Low-Sensory Library Spaces

Libraries tend to be bright primary-colored bulletin-board-filled spaces that are designed to encourage the public, especially

DOI: 10.4324/9781003185369-16

children, to engage with reading. While this can create a fun and stimulating environment, it can also be a challenging experience for a person with autism. One way to help make your library more accessible is to offer a low-sensory less stimulating space. The simplest description of a low-sensory area in a library setting is a room or a quiet corner where a reader is able to take a break from the environmental stimuli. Please note that a low-sensory space is different from a sensory space. A sensory space is designed to engage the senses, and a low-sensory space is created to be calm and peaceful. If your library has the ability to dedicate a room specifically for this use, this is the best option. While that may not be possible, because sometimes there is limited space, I suggest then that a multipurpose room have a low-sensory component or area.

The first step in designing a low-sensory space is to identify the room or the area and then label it for the public. We don't want the sensory space to look or feel like a play room as this may restrict the usage for people who need the area for a quiet moment. A reading room is often a better fit if the room is multiuse. Signage for the space should include some visuals and provide some basic directions. The physical space itself might include things like beanbag chairs or soft comfortable sofas to sit on. It should also include a lighting design that allows for flexibility, including the ability to dim the lights and always have harsh overhead lighting. It is important to consider ambient noise in the space as libraries sometimes have computers and air-conditioning systems that might hum or make other sounds. When possible, it is advisable to place a low- sensory space away from those types of noise-making objects. The space need not be too large, as you don't want it to fill up with multiple people. Options for fidgets or other handheld items to help individuals express their feelings would be useful in such a space. If the library has the budget, offering noise-cancelling headphones is a nice option. It may also be helpful to have a stack of blankets or a mat on the floor in case a child would like to lie down for a few moments.

Some libraries require that a family sign up for a time slot in the space; however, this has the potential to limit the accessibility when someone is having an unscheduled moment and just needs five or ten minutes in the space. Other libraries take the next steps and might incorporate the option for soothing music, or even tactile items on the walls. It is also important to consider a child's safety in such a space, and be sure that anything that is accessible is soft and that safety items like outlet covers are in place, and furniture does not have any sharp corners.

Sensory-Friendly Browsing

One method of improving access to readers at your library is to offer sensory-friendly browsing hours. These hours take place outside of the hours for the general public. This strategy is often utilized as a way to encourage individuals and families to come into the library. Too frequently, a library will put these hours at one particular time of the day, which can be quite limiting for a family. For example, some libraries that open at 9 AM in the morning will have 8 AM to 9 AM as the time for sensory-friendly browsing. However, this may be a part of the day when a child is not yet awake, or in the middle of a breakfast or morning routine. It is important when choosing these hours and creating your schedule that there are several options. It may be that one day a week is early in the morning, but there are other days that offer times in the evenings. This will allow for more people to participate.

Autism Friendly Programming

There are many libraries that are offering Autism Friendly programming. While we are going to discuss some options for these programs, please remember what was mentioned previously in this book - that inclusion means everyone, and that while these activities can be beneficial, they are segregating a specific population from others. The best practice is to incorporate strategies and supports into programming that is offered to everybody, and make it a truly neurodiverse environment. The suggestions made here can be utilized for both types of programs. A sample registration form is provided and is specific for a children's program. It can be modified depending on the type of activity you are offering.

*Sample Autism Friendly Program Registration Form

Information Form

Child's name: _____

Parent name: _____

What is your child's diagnosis or area of support needs?

_____

What is your child's learning style (circle one)?

Visual   Auditory   Experiential   Other _____

What is your child's primary method of communication?

_____

Do you have concerns for your child's safety? (Please let us know how we can support your child.)

_____

What is your child's most comfortable learning setting? (circle one)

One-on-one learning   Small group learning   Large group learning

What are your child's strengths, interests, or hobbies?

_____

Does your child have any behavioral concerns that you would like to make us aware of?

_____

What areas do you suspect your child will require some assistance with?

☐ Adhering to the schedule   ☐ Understanding the activity   ☐ Attention

☐ Following Directions   ☐ Social Interaction   ☐ Motor Skills

Is there any information that you would like to share to help us know your child better?

_____

Will you or another caregiver be present for the program? If so, please indicate who will be attending.

_____

Sensory-Friendly Movie Night

A movie night can be a fun outing for a child, teen, or adult. Since we are discussing libraries, considering pairing a movie and a book together to offer a movie activity. Introduce the book and provide different reading and literacy level options for participants. These can range from picture books to graphic novels to complete works to audio books. This way your participants may participate on the book side of the event regardless of their reading level or ability. When showing the movie, some suggestions are to have the lights on in the theatre space, to have the volume of the film at a slightly quieter level, and to provide many options for seating that go beyond folding chairs, such as sofas, mats, and blankets.

A nice way to incorporate some autism-specific strategies would be to design a social story about going to see the movie and to also create a heads-up-type playbill that informs viewers where loud noises or unexpected scenes may happen in the movie. It is also helpful to remind families of where the low-sensory space or quiet room in your library is in case an individual needs to take a break and to also set some ground rules for physicality during the movie. This could be that people can stand up at any point in the movie but they are directed to not walk in front of the screen or projector, or that if they need to walk around during the film that there is a space provided toward the back or the side of the theatre. It is also an option to suggest to families that they bring their own pillows, blankets, and food, if food is allowed in the space. Also be sure to consider potential developmental levels of the viewers, and when advertising the movie target your audience by indicating not only the type of movie but also if the movie contains explicit language or violence.

Sensory-Friendly Story Time

Sensory-friendly story hour or story time is very popular in libraries. These activities are typically during the week days for children who are home-schooled or they are on Saturday mornings. Sensory-friendly story hour can be an excellent introduction to the library for children. It is an opportunity for them to be in a space with other children who are their peers and to have social interaction while learning about books. This type of program should be developed with some goals in mind. Is the goal of the experience to simply bring people into the library setting, or is it for learning or developing a specific interest? Some sensory-friendly story hours are highly sensory. They utilize the experience in a book and then amplify it to be interactive. An example of this is utilizing a bubble machine while reading a book about sea creatures. Perhaps also passing around shells that have different textures, and maybe including stuffed animals or puppets that are the type of fish in the book. These types of experiences can be very engaging. A lower sensory story hour might be one where the lights are dim, the children sit on mats or blankets on the floor, and a more soothing type of story is read slowly and at a lower volume. It is important to distinguish between sensory level and presentation when marketing this type of event so that families know what to expect.

All sensory-friendly events should have options for a quiet or a break space and for plenty of room for the child to move around. These activities also have the opportunity to show children and families the children's section of the library and to possibly encourage children to become a library card holder or to check out a book before or after the program. If library staff feel like they need support in developing these programs, especially if there is a particular curricular outcome goal, it can be helpful to engage an autism specialist, specifically those who have experience as a Speech Language Pathologist.

Chapter 14

Summer Camp Inclusion and IRPs

Summer camp can be a life-changing experience for children. It offers them the opportunity to be independent of their parents, and to connect with peers their own age, while being outdoors and doing activities that are not available in a school, classroom, or home setting. Often the friendships and affinity from camp programs are lifelong. As a camper alumnus myself, my summers at camp were some of the most important ones in my life. Often, when the families I've worked with have children that attend camp, they are changed from the experience, having more independence and a broadened scope of interests.

When designing an neurodiverse summer camp experience, creating a staff position for inclusion is essential. Many camps now have a full-time inclusion specialist who focuses on diversity and disability. If your program is unable to fund such a position, then it is essential to have at least one point-person or someone at the director level who has this kind of training. Ideally, this individual will have a background in Special Education, behavior, or neurodiversity.

All staff who are working with children in the camp setting should be trained. A basic overview of autism is essential for everyone, from the cook to the counselors, as they are likely to connect with these children in at least some capacity. For counselors and program staff who will be working more closely with children, having an in-depth training is important. This training should focus on communication, behavior, safety, and how to help support any needs that arise.

For camp programs specialists that feel overwhelmed by the prospect full inclusion, there are other ways to support children in your camp without necessarily taking on the extent of the education and experience that might be needed. For example, one option is to bring in experts who have experience working with children who have high support needs and having them be those children's one-on-one or support person. You can hire them directly, or utilize their services as a consultant. This is a way to offer an inclusive program in your city while integrating professionals with a high level of knowledge.

When enrolling children into camps, the standard camp form should include a few key questions about the needs of the child, specifically about safety issues, elopement, behavioral concerns, and preferred communication method. The answers to those questions should be followed up by an in-depth review, a conversation with the child, the parents, and caregivers, at the start of the IRP process. At the City of Boynton Beach, Stephanie Soplop, who was the Recreation Program Specialist, created the IRP, which stands for Individual Recreation Plan. An IRP is modeled after an IEP which is an educational plan typically used in Special

Education in the United States. A sample of an IRP is shown here. The IRP identifies the child, their emergency contact information, their interests and likes, any challenges and limitations they may have, and it outlines strategies. The strategies are in direct response to the support needs of the child. It leaves rooms for comments and for parent and guardian signature, as well as a signature by the camp.

Other aspects of an inclusionary summer camp program are to have frequent observations of how the child is doing and to adjust the IRP based on that data. It is possible that the assumed needs at the beginning of the program will change over time once the child becomes comfortable in the setting. Visual supports, social stories, and other strategies are also useful to incorporate into camp programs, and can be developed for specific aspects of the experience. For example, a social story about the first day at the camp would be useful, but also creating social stories about the first time on a boat, or a visual support on how to make s'mores over a campfire, can help a child feel prepared and more comfortable engaging in new experiences.

*IRP (Individualized Recreational Program)

City of Boynton Beach
Recreation & Parks Department

Individualized Recreational Program (IRP) Plan

Participant's Name: Participant's Age:

Parent/Guardian Name: Home Phone:
Work Phone: Cell Phone:

Parent/Guardian Name: Home Phone:
Work Phone: Cell Phone:

Challenges/Limitations: Difficulties with transitions and sensitivity to loud noise

Strategies

Use prompts prior to transitions to different activities, being clear and specific:
In 10 minutes we will be lining up at the front of the room. In 5 minutes I will be calling everyone at this table to line up.

Use transition cues:
Visual timer/countdown
Auible Timer (Play music and prompt that when the music stops playing it is time to line up or vice versa)

Provide a warning before loud activities (loud music while practicing for talent show, etc.)

To encourrage camper to participate in group activities, have her be a helper at first (score keeper, assist with setting up for the activity, etc.) and then slowly encourage her to participate a little bit at a time.

Comments:

_____

_____

_____

Parent/Guardian   Print Name   Signature   Date

Recreation Supervisor   Print Name   Signature   Date

Chapter 15

Employment and HR Tips

While this book primarily focuses on the needs of residents living in a city, there are definitely going to be people with autism who are city employees, or who want to work for your city. It is useful to briefly touch upon this here and for human resource departments to consider at least a few small modifications to their typical hiring process in order to improve and develop inclusionary practice.

One of the most simple and straightforward ways to make change or to make sure you are well informed about employee accommodations is to utilize the United States Department of Labor's Office of Disability Employment Policy (ODEP) JAN the Job Accommodation Network. JAN, which can be found at https://askjan.org This website provides excellent information and even a help line to support employers in determining potential accommodations for the workplace. They have search criteria by disability and situation. They suggest resources and accommodations to support the employee in completing essential functions of the job which include:

DOI: 10.4324/9781003185369-18

- Equipment
- Environmental modifications
- Flexible scheduling
- Modifying job tasks
- Unique solutions such as rehabilitation engineering evaluations

Other ways to improve inclusion is to be open and flexible in modifying some of your standardized processes, especially around hiring. Job interviews are a very social and verbal activity. For people with autism, these can be times where they experience difficulty. Consider some very simple changes to how you interview. One alteration I recommend is to provide the interview questions to the individual ahead of time. We may think that interview questions are supposed to be a surprise and something that we need to come up with answers for on the spot; but the majority of the questions we ask include things like what are our goals in five years, and why do we want this particular position. These are questions that are important for people to have time to put some thought into, and it is likely that you will receive a more thoroughly developed response if the questions are provided. Also, having the questions printed out and available in front of the person during the interview can be very helpful. Another area to be flexible is that applicants may not have a traditional résumé. Their résumé could be functional or could be a video résumé or portfolio that shows them completing the job task versus a resume that describes those tasks. These type of resumes are used very commonly in the disability community and should be received with the same amount of respect and consideration as a paper résumé.

If you are in the United States, there is a national program called Vocational Rehabilitation. This program helps people with disabilities obtain and maintain employment. They can provide job coaching and support needed in the workplace. If you are having difficulty meeting the accommodation needs of an employee, for example, if they require an adjustable desk and it is not in your budget, it is possible that Vocational Rehabilitation may provide funding for such an item. There are many resources to support people with disabilities in the workplace, and it's important to have a good understanding of what is available.

Chapter 16

Conclusion:
Share with Others

If your actions create a legacy that inspires others to
dream more, learn more, do more and become more,
then you are an excellent leader.

– Dolly Parton

The Autism Friendly movement can only grow if we share our
experiences with others. Start small. Celebrate wins. Observe
those you are impacting and take the time to embrace the
change that happens in your city. If those moments touch
your heart and light a fire in you, you will understand those
who are making this movement the mission of their careers
and their lives, and hopefully, you will join them. Listen to the
cities that have created spaces like barrier-free parks, feature
artists with autism in their cultural centers and public places,
and who hire neurodiverse interns or develop mentoring programs. Grow from their experience and challenge yourself and
others to have new and innovative ideas that will continue to
develop this perspective. Engage with those outside of your

DOI: 10.4324/9781003185369-19

city and with the larger disability community. Establish official policies and procedures that support the continuance of this work in case you leave your city position or employer. Create community work groups and conferences that highlight your efforts and gift your strategies to others. Tell your story while it flourishes.

Determining You Are an Autism Friendly City

While there are organizations and consultants who can provide you with a designation that indicates you are an Autism Friendly City, it is something you and your residents need to decide for yourself as you choose to announce it to the community. You might wonder if you've done enough, but know that there will always be more to do. Feel comfortable in receiving ongoing and long-term feedback from your Inclusion Team, as they will continue to be there for you over time. Consider these questions to determine if you've completed enough steps and had enough impact to say that you are an Autism Friendly City:

1. Have all city staff completed a training that provided at least a general overview of autism?
2. Did staff that work closely with neurodiverse individuals complete a more in-depth autism training?
3. What strategies (i.e. social stories and visual supports) did your city implement?
4. Are implemented strategies being utilized and are they effective?
5. Are city residents aware of your initiative, and do they indicate that accessibility has increased and barriers decreased?
6. Did you develop an Inclusion Team and do they continue to consult with your city to provide guidance and feedback?
7. Do you have a plan in place to maintain the strategies and supports you developed?

Declaring You Are an Autism Friendly City

There are many creative and unique ways to tell others that you are Autism Friendly City. Some cities will start with a press release, newspaper article, or media story. Others will work with their city leaders and create a proclamation or specialized announcement at a city commission or town hall meeting. Some cities will develop a logo, or secondary graphic, that indicates they are autism or disability friendly. Others will develop a certificate or plaque that hangs in city hall. A fun way to share at your city is that Autism Friendly is to wrap your vehicles, such as police cars, in graphics that highlight your city's commitment. Many cities will include Autism Friendly indicators on their car bumpers or the side doors of their service cars, or even on their emergency medical vehicles. You can include an Autism Friendly graphic or logo on all of your city staff's email signatures. Consider having ribbon cutting with your Inclusion Team. There are even cities that will develop a short video explaining how and why they are now Autism Friendly, and share that on their social media. I've seen cities create t-shirts that their team members wear during certain times of the year. Some cities will create a website or social media page that showcase their Autism Friendly City and tells the story of what they did, and the changes they made, strategies implemented, and what their plans are for the future. The possibilities are endless.

Success Stories

Share your success stories to demonstrate evidence of proof of concept. They are validation of how an idea works after it is implemented, and the impact on the intended population. Success stories are also an excellent way of highlighting an individual or group's contribution to the community.

Some success stories might focus on a specific individual with autism, a child, family, or even a city employee. They might feature a support that the city provided, or a new strategy that opened up accessibility and improved quality of service experienced by a resident. For example, if a swimming program became inclusive, where in the past it might not have been able to accommodate a child with autism, it could be viewed as a success story for the child, family, and city.

Other success stories might include when an individual with autism gains employment at the city. Perhaps that person has always dreamed of being a camp counselor, a professional in the city administrative department, or a first responder. The city team has learned about inclusive practice, and they hired that individual, perhaps supporting that individual's needs by providing some supports on the job. Other types of success might include reporting about city events that are disability-specific or highly inclusive. Another type of success story might be featuring newly developed programs or when a social story or specialized visual support is created. Success can come from inside the city walls, or from those that reside in the town, but the only way for your residents and community to know the effect of your initiative is to tell others.

Conference/Expo

Several years ago, I recognized the importance of having cities and organizations that had developed Autism Friendly practices share their experiences with others. In response to this need, I developed and hosted the world's only known Autism Friendly Cities Institute at FAU's Center for Autism and Related Disabilities. At this conference, city leaders are able to share the ways in which they have implemented strategies to make their town more neurodiverse and inclusive. The institute started small, but even in the early days, attendees came from distant counties and left with ideas and concepts worth considering. The participants in these institutes were city staff and leaders, who included human resource managers, managers, recreation program staff, and city commissioners. The conference has varied from year to year as new types of implementation are brought forward. Typically, it includes one keynote speaker, a panel of representatives from various city or community projects, and a I provide a brief update where I share some general strategies for those new to the initiative, and I highlight innovation that has come into light over the past year. Keynote presenters have included the City of Boynton Beach, a police sergeant from the City of Jupiter who was sharing their autism 911 registry program, as well as Dr. Toby Honsberger, who was the coordinator of an Autism Friendly nature area. I've found it useful to have a panel at these institutes to encourage conversation and to bring more voices to the table. Panels have ranged from three or four to six representatives who are doing something new in the community or who have a different perspective. It is especially useful for these panels to include a person with autism who has been directly impacted by either a strategy or a program. It is helpful to highlight how it has been valuable in their life and why it has made a difference for them.

These conferences can be offered with minimal expense or can be sponsored by local organizations. Feature individuals who are implementing strategies and who are willing to share their stories without charging speaker costs. Offer them a marketing opportunity or an exchange that will be a way to support their needs, such as providing them a table to give away flyers about their upcoming programs. During COVID-19 times, our institute moved online, and while it was a different feel than an in-person experience, the numbers of people who were able to participate, and the expanded distance from which they were able to engage, definitely magnified our reach. Utilizing a conference format to share information has been markedly successful as I've seen firsthand that attendees have taken information back to their own cities and implemented what they learned.

Thank You

If you've gotten this far, I thank you for your interest and for considering bringing the Autism Friendly Movement to your city. I hope that these pages provided you with guidance, thought-provoking questions, and solutions. If you worked through this book as you brought a neurodiverse perspective to your city, I congratulate you for your dedication to making your city more inclusive and accessible. If you haven't started the process yet, I encourage you to take the initial step, even if it is a small one, and to experience first-hand how even minor changes can impact and improve the quality of life for another.

Appendix: Implementation Examples

What you do makes a difference, and you have to decide what kind of difference you want to make.

– Jane Goodall

The following examples are based on real-world experiences. Different cities and communities created the following events, products, services, and initiatives. While they may have personalized them to meet the needs of their own residents, they are models of how to implement strategies for access and inclusion. Samples are provided within the examples, as available. Please modify them to fit your needs.

Emergency Registry

When an individual makes a call for emergency assistance, basic information such as the person's location will typically register on the computer of the receiving operator. While this is a useful aid to locate someone, it provides no other helpful information. If the person is calling for help, in the region they live, a 911/999 Emergency Registry can support a better experience for both the family requesting the assistance, and the first responders who arrive on the scene. While registries are completely voluntary, they are appreciated and sought after, especially by parents of children with autism who frequently elope.

Some cities may already have a version of this type of registry that they utilize for older adults who have dementia or other cognitive concerns. It might be easiest to modify and adapt your current templates and use them for this purpose. For cities that do not have an Emergency Registry, it can be something relatively easy to create and incorporate into the address and location features of your emergency response system.

The important information to gather is the individual's name, identifying features, their age, their primary method of communication, what may frighten or scare them if approached, and where they are likely to go when they elope. When requesting information about the individual's primary method of communication, it may be useful to ask whether or not they are verbal or nonverbal, and if they have basic literacy skills. If your emergency system allows for photographs, that can also be very helpful. It is important that families update this information on a regular basis, and it is suggested that this is done annually. When a family calls emergency response and the first responder in the field can bring up all of these details, the odds of locating a child or adult more quickly increase. The information on any specific locations they tend to go when they leave their home or school unsupervised is essential. Families can note if there are water hazards nearby. These details can support first responders and guide them with an initial direction to start their search. Locations may include places like the neighborhood playground, pools or other bodies of water, friends' homes, or buildings they are familiar with, such as school. A person with autism may not be cautious about crossing the road or may enter the water without knowing how to swim or be safe, especially if they are experiencing agitation. Having this information ahead of time that can help identify the individual, and knowing where they may to elope to can potentially save a life.

An Artist Illustrates the City Calendar

As the Autism Friendly Cities program at the City of Boynton Beach expanded, they were interested in connecting with an individual with autism who could bring their talents to a city project. When they started brainstorming ideas, they were unsure of how to locate such a person. They turned to their Inclusion Team for suggestions and discovered a Familial Entrepreneurship called Artists with Autism (www .artistswithautism.com). The city reached out and connected with artist Brandon Drucker. After discussions with him, it was agreed that Brandon would use his artistic abilities to illustrate the annual calendar published by the city. Not only would Brandon illustrate the cover, but he would also provide art for every month of the calendar. To make the calendar more locally focused, Brandon created images of the city's intracoastal park, Italian ice and creamery shop, and the marina. The calendar was an extraordinary success, and the city published and distributed a massive 75,000 copies. The calendar was entered into a nationwide competition where it won second place out of over 700 submissions. Brandon was recognized at a public meeting by the city commission. At that gathering, a woman who creates quilts saw the calendar and offered to print the art onto fabric and sew it into a quilt. The quilt had the panels from each of the different months of the calendar, and after it was acknowledged by the city, the quilt was displayed in the City of Boynton Beach's main atrium that year. The city calendar, illustrated by Brandon, is a powerful example of how to highlight the talents of a person with autism who lives in your city, through a creative collaboration. This demonstrates your city's commitment to celebrating neurodiversity and supports a local artist, sharing their talents with the community.

Autism Friendly Nature Area

Natural areas, forest preserves, estuaries, conservation parks, and wildlife sanctuaries, are frequently part of city spaces that fall under the auspices of a park and recreation or public works department. These nature areas are beautiful and inviting, but also have many safety concerns for individuals with autism. The most troubling is water. According to the Autism Society of Florida, *children with autism are 160 times more likely to experience nonfatal and fatal drowning than their neurotypical peers, and in the State of Florida, the number one cause of death for people with autism is drowning* (www .autismfl.org/drowning-prevention). There are many ways to enhance safety measures throughout these natural spaces without compromising the environmental appeal.

In South Florida, a natural area was designed to be Autism Friendly by Dr. Toby Honsberger from The Learning Academy at the Els Center of Excellence in collaboration with the Palm Beach County Department of Environmental Resource Management and the North Jupiter Flatwoods Natural Area. The Autism Friendly experience begins on the Learning Academy's website: http://tlacad.org/flatwoods/, where visitors can explore the nature area through an interactive virtual tour. This is extremely valuable for individuals who might want to know what a place looks like before they choose to visit. A second virtual experience on the site, is the social story and narrative that they developed. The social story brings participants through the park section by section with pictures and first-person text that describes what they will see and experience. It also includes some basic rules and suggestions for navigating areas that may have safety concerns. A second version of the social story is offered that includes symbols and icons for those who have limited reading abilities. There is a section on the website where trail rules are clearly indicated. To enhance the natural area, they also developed a nature trail guide and sensory scavenger hunts.

In the nature area there are paved paths that provide boundaries for walking and enjoying the space. There are visual supports incorporated into the signage. There are frequent benches that allow for resting throughout the trails. They've also incorporated a swing and sensory stations to encourage tactile engagement with the space. Physical barriers were installed near water areas and other places that have safety concerns, and a map is provided that is clear about where each path leads, the distance of each trail, where the rest areas are, bathroom locations, and what is available to interact with on the exploration. The thought put into this Autism Friendly nature area was extensive, and the natural areas is utilized by adults, children, families, and local schools.

Inclusive/Barrier-Free Playground

Playgrounds are designed to be enjoyed by children. A child should not have the experience of going to the park and not being able to play. However, many recreation areas contain barriers for individuals with autism, and the result is that they are unable to fully participate.

Barrier-free parks are a way to increase accessibility and safety, and to offer a play place for all children. Many parks have obstacles that prevent accessibility for people with autism. There are ways to remove those impediments and improve ease of use. Safety is the primary factor that needs to be considered when developing an Autism Friendly playground. Water hazards must be considered a primary concern. If the park is near open water, a swamp, or river, it is essential to develop measures that will detour a person with autism so they cannot access the water in an unsafe way. This may be done with fencing, strategically placed bushes, visual signage, and even changes to the texture of a path to indicate that something potentially unsafe is coming. Also, any social stories or visuals that are created related to the playground experience need to identify any potential water hazards that an adult, parent, or caregiver might need to be aware of. Safety concerns also include the placement of playgrounds in relation to roads, parking lots, and other motorized vehicles. If a road must be crossed, including visual and audio crossing supports into the available technology can be helpful. If the playground is near sports venues or other activity areas, be aware of safety related to large crowds or physical hazards.

Another aspect to consider is the flow of the playground. In many recreation areas, all of the activities are bunched together, which creates excessive of stimuli, especially if there are several children using the same piece of equipment. One way to help mitigate this is to create sections that are separated to provide more physical space but with opportunities to be together in the same general area. Playground equipment itself can become more accessible when things like height and weight restrictions are increased. There may be a teenager with autism who really likes to swing, but if the swing is designed for a five-year-old child, then it becomes an activity that is no longer accessible to a teen or adult. It is important to recognize that neurodiverse individuals may be at different developmental stages and that the facilities at your playground should be accessible to all people of all ages.

When designing the surface of the ground at your play area, consider texture. Is the terrain going to be concrete or cement, or will there be natural grass or a rubberized surface? The ground type can impact level of injury if there is a fall and can influence the amount of heat on a playground.

Some regions may have fewer choices because they need to utilize certain materials for their climate. Recognize that different types of textures can also create a sensory reaction for someone. For example, if a path to a playground is lined with small stones, the experience of stepping on the rocks and the sound of those rocks may be painful or uncomfortable. Ground types, paint colors, and shapes can also be utilized as visual supports by designing with different types of materials that indicate where to play, where to sit and rest, and used to designate the entrances, exists, and safety hazards. It is also important to note that bathrooms can offer more than what is required by the general ADA requirements. They can be enhanced with things like toilet seats that turn, bathroom chairs that are incorporated in to the walls, and several extra-large stalls to allow for a support person to be in the space with an individual.

Offering a quiet space that is lower sensory at a playground is also useful. It might be slightly away from the main play area, and would be best to be in a type of pavilion that provides shade and coverage from weather. It can include a comfortable place to sit, should an individual or family need a few minutes away from the action. When barrier free playgrounds are constructed with all visitors in mind, there are many ways to utilize design to support accessibility for anyone who wants to play.

Autism Day of Fun

One way to support the autistic residents in your community is to create an Autism Day of Fun. These types of events are titled differently depending on where you are located, and they can range from a family fun day to a day for autism to an autism walk to awesome for autism day. People get very creative in naming their events.

An Autism Day of Fun event typically includes your local autism-related agencies, support organizations, and service providers. Sometimes these events are developed to provide fundraising for these groups. The event may feature music, showcase firefighting trucks and equipment, bringing out police cruisers out for children to see, and possibly even a demonstration by the police canine unit. Interactive activities might include arts and crafts, games, a bounce house, or even a chance to meet a local celebrity or famous person who visits with families.

If your event includes a walk or 5K, it is helpful to create a couple of different options for individuals and families. Sometimes there will be a traditional 5K and a secondary walk, of perhaps one lap around a park or a shorter designated area. When determining time of year for this type of event, be sure to consider the weather, and how that might impact having people outside for long periods of time.

Typically, the agencies and groups involved with fun days will have some sort of resource aspect to this type of day and will often offer flyers, brochures, and giveaways that are related to their services. When developing these types of events, it is important to ask your local experts to provide some of the activities as they may be doing this as part of their practices and it would be useful to have activities planned by people with a strong background in autism. This is also a chance to integrate your local social enterprises and family entrepreneurs, so that they can sell their goods and be included in their community. The preparation for family fun days should include implementing safety precautions and utilizing event planning strategies for inclusive programs is important. Sometimes events are held at a park or natural area and the organizers don't recognize that they have just asked 100 children with autism to play 20 feet from a pond. It is essential to choose spaces responsibly and that safety is a number one concern. This is also a great opportunity to utilize the experience and expertise of your Inclusion

Team as they can provide feedback and offer suggestions related to safety and planning.

Family fun days are also opportunities that are useful for businesses that might be Autism Friendly to showcase some of the ways that they are creating supports and implementing innovative ideas. For example, in my region there is a business that developed a sensory-friendly bounce house. They spent many years designing this inflatable and received input from local autism specialists and families. Sometimes these types of events are incorporated into holiday activities. For example, there are cities that offer a sensory-friendly visit with Santa, a Thanksgiving meal, or an Easter egg hunt. These are ways to connect with families during special times of the year.

Family fun days can offer opportunities for families with similar experiences and needs to gather. When your city facilitates ways of bringing families together, within a fun and social event, structuring and incorporating time for parents and children to meet and connect with each other can be a valuable opportunity for groups with similar needs to develop natural supports and friendships.

Outreach and Giveaways

Everyone enjoys getting something for free. While that is nice, it is helpful when a giveaway is also useful. It can be a win-win when it is valuable to both the giver and the receiver. When connecting with families in your local community, there are things that can be given from the city to residents, which are beneficial for everybody. Most of these types of giveaways revolve around safety, and the items can easily be purchased online or developed in-house. They can be given away in groups, sets, kits, or as individual items that are offered at public events. Some giveaways may be things that police officers and other first responders have in their possession for times when they connect with families or individuals with autism.

There are many more items than those that are being suggested here; however, this should give you a place to start, and a way to brainstorm what may be needed that is specific to the needs of your city.

- Resource Packet: Information about swim lessons, mental health services, emergency phone numbers, and your community's crisis line. This literature can be printed in full, or created in a digital format to save paper and costs, with a giveaway that includes the website or QR code.

- Magnets: Emergency numbers for the local crisis line or places like poison control can be created and shared.

- Fire Decals: Companies make glow in the dark fire stickers that are typically placed on or near the front door of a home as well as near the bedroom door of an individual with autism. The decals indicate that a person with autism lives in the home, and they can help a firefighter locate an autistic person within the home.

- Seatbelt ID Card Holder: Several companies and creative sellers on sites like Etsy sell small card holders that attach to a seatbelt. These are useful to provide information to a first responder when there is a car accident or other vehicle-related response. A person with autism can have a card on their seatbelt, indicating they have autism, and sharing their name, age, communication preferences, needs, and any medical information that the person may not be able to express during an emergency.

- Wallet Card Information: The Wallet Card is a program through The Disability Independence Group, designed in conjunction with the Coral Gables Police and University of Miami/Nova Southeastern Center for Autism and

Related Disabilities. The purpose of a wallet card is for an individual with autism, a child or adult, to have a card that they carry on their person that indicates their name, disability, age, verbal ability, contact information, and emergency contact numbers. There is also the opportunity to add customized information. The Wallet Card has no cost and is a way to have an item that identifies that a person has autism, without putting the indicator on a driver's license or state ID. On the website there is a video explaining the usefulness of the wallet card: https://www.justdigit.org/wallet-cards/

■ Pool Watcher Tags: These tags, created with a laminated card and lanyard to go around one's neck or body, are used to identify the responsible adult who is tasked with watching people swimming in a pool or body of water. These are used during a group gathering at a home or community pool that does not have a lifeguard. These tags are extremely helpful, especially if the gathering includes loud music, many people, and alcohol consumption. When drownings happen, the adults often believe that there was someone who was supposed to be the pool watcher, but it is rarely clear who that person was. These tags can eliminate confusion and prevent tragedy.

■ Electric Wireless Door Alarms: Door alarms are an essential safety item for families that have a child or adult with autism who elopes. These small, inexpensive, battery-operated door alarms can alert a parent or caregiver that an individual has successfully opened a door and has possibly exited. They are useful in homes and for families that travel. Utilizing a door alarm can prevent a person from being in danger.

■ Stop Signs: Adhesive small stop signs can be used by families as visual supports to prevent a person from entering an area that is unsafe for them, or opening a cabinet or door that leads to items that could injure a person. Stop signs are typically laminated pieces of card stock so they can be re-used as needed.

- Safety Proofing Items: Safety proofing items can prevent an injury in the home. We may call some of these child-proofing items, but it is possible that they will be needed in a residence where an individual with autism is a teen or adult. Items include corner guards for sharp furniture edges, safety locks for cabinets and closets that may contain poisonous items, door knob covers, appliance or stove locks, and guards or covers for electrical outlets. These items are often small and inexpensive. They can be purchased at just about any home goods or large box stores. They can be given out at safety events or as part of a safety kit.

- Books on Safety: It is a nice gesture to include books in giveaway boxes or bags. These books can range in topics, but there are many safety-focused books that that are created specifically for children, teens, and adults . These books might include stories about pool safety, fire safety, and stranger danger. There are many organizations that give these books away for no cost, or they can be purchased in bulk for a reasonable amount. It may be useful to find some that are location-specific to your city. For example, in the Florida region, offering a book about hurricane safety would be relatable and appropriate.

Emergency Shelters

There are a variety of situations that can cause a need for your residents to access emergency shelters. Conditions might include a hurricane, earthquake, flood, significant power outage, bad weather, or other natural disasters. In these situations, shelter staff may be volunteers or public employees who could be working outside of their typical scope of work. It will be essential to make sure they have training. At the very least, they need basic information on autism, as well as how people with autism may respond to an emergency. This training or information should include simple strategies and techniques that they can implement in a shelter environment.

Materials can be supplied to shelters to improve the experience for individuals with autism and their families. Comfort items include blankets, pillows, and stuffed animals. Shelters should also be supplied with earplugs, headphones, and fidget items to help with overstimulation. If a gymnasium is being used as a shelter, gym mats can be used to create a cushioned area. However, that type of space may reverberate sound, and if classrooms or other smaller areas can be offered to a family, that may help them have a space with less stimuli. Sensory bags, games, and pre-charged electronic devices that don't require the internet can help with engagement and distraction from a potentially stressful environment. Social stories and visual supports should also be created to provide to families when they register or when they arrive at the location.

Support Social Enterprise and Familial Entrepreneurship

One manner of increasing connection to people with autism is to reach out to your local social enterprises. You may not realize, but frequently there are many businesses and programs that are either run by or have employees with autism and other disabilities. A good place to start looking for these types of businesses is to ask your Inclusion Team what they are aware of and possibly work with. Some of these social enterprises will exist within schools, transition or independent living programs, or they may be independent businesses started by relatives of individuals with autism, known as Familial Entrepreneurships.

Some examples of social enterprises and familial entrepreneurship, local to South Florida, are ScentsAbility Candles and The Chocolate Spectrum. These two businesses were started by mothers in order to provide employment and social opportunities for their adult children who have developmental disabilities. Both the businesses are thriving and now employ several individuals with disabilities, as well as provide vocational training opportunities and life skills. The Chocolate Spectrum (www.thechocolatespectrum.com/) is a gourmet chocolate company that can individualize and design chocolate treats for any occasion. ScentsAbility Candles (www.scentsability.org/) is a candle company that creates unique and beautiful candles which can be enjoyed at home or used as corporate or event gifts and giveaways. There are many entrepreneurship programs that exist within schools, and locally, that includes students who make organic dog treats, one that bakes cookies, and at another school they have a woodworking shop where every holiday season they create large reindeer that are offered for sale as winter decoration. At the majority of these businesses and programs, funds that are received are allocated back into the program or utilized as salaries for the employees.

There are many opportunities to include these types of businesses in your city. Instead of buying pens, signs, brochures, or gifts from a corporate entity, look to see if there are social enterprises near you that can offer similar products. This way your city will connect with a business or program that employs people with autism, and you can establish a relationship with this type of business. Participating individuals may want to join your Inclusion Team. These opportunities are a win-win as you expand your connection to the autism community, while you support businesses by making a purchase that is socially responsible and celebrates the skills and talents of your own city residents. These pictures show a candle from ScentsAbility Candle and a box of chocolate confections from The Chocolate Spectrum.

Agency Fair

A beneficial way to support your local disability programs, organizations, and service providers is to host an agency fair. This helps them share what they to offer with the community and is an opportunity for your residents to learn about what resources are available for them. This type of event can be offered as a sole event where it is focused specifically on your local nonprofits, or it can be done in association with one of your annual events or a specialized event that is targeted for the disability community. For example, Touch a Truck is an event that many cities have to help children become more familiar with emergency responders, including firefighters, medical personnel, and police officers. This is an excellent chance for individuals with autism to be able to interact with those professionals and safety officers they may come into contact with in their community, as well as an opportunity to offer an agency or program fair as part of the event.

The agency fair aspect of this type of event would include setting out tables and tents (if outside) for different agency representatives to share information about their programs, and to allow them to pass out their materials to your local residents. A city might provide a cloth bag or backpack for participants to use to hold all the items they collect, and for the city to include some of their materials about services or information on upcoming events. These type of programs can be extremely beneficial as they bring agencies together that might be housed slightly further outside of your community, but that serve your residents, and that brings a representative from that program directly to your residents. Agency fairs typically have minimal cost and can be both educational and fun for your city.

First Responder Event

Community events, where residents and first responders come together in an informal environment, can help decrease some of the stigma that may be associated with an encounter out in the community. A way to help make this type of event more disability friendly would be to follow some of the suggestions in the event planning portion of this book but also to include opportunities for first responders to talk through and possibly even demonstrate some of what happens when they are called out to a scene. For example, a firefighter might show how they use the hose, or the police unit might bring out their search dogs to meet the public. For older children and teens, including some adults, it can be an opportunity to help them with some of the independent living skills related to emergencies that they might be concerned about, for example, putting together a checklist of how to respond after a car accident driving. This might be something to create with some guidance from law enforcement. Another option could be screening a safety movie together, such as Be Safe the Movie, which reviews appropriate ways to interact with law enforcement. Here is the link to the movie's website, and a short description from that site: https://besafethemovie.com

> What would your son, daughter or student do in an encounter with the police? Run? Fight? Melt down? Those are scary possibilities. More news stories than ever focus attention on individuals with disabilities who have unsafe or even disastrous encounters with law enforcement. Now is the time to help young people with autism or other learning differences learn the skills they need to interact safely with the police. BE SAFE the Movie and BE SAFE Teaching Edition are the indispensable teaching tools you've been looking for! The BE SAFE video modelling program shows teens and adults what to do in everyday situations with the police. Actors with autism and other disabilities interact with real police officers, modelling safe words and actions. Whether it is being pulled over while driving or following instructions from the police, the 1-hour BE SAFE DVD teaches life-saving skills that everyone needs to know!

Economic/Business Initiative

Bringing your community businesses together can be a good way of deepening the commitment and broadening the scope of your Autism Friendly City initiative. Inclusion programs that create partnerships with local companies are one way to accomplish this. These partnerships will require training and education for business owners and their employees. The businesses themselves can implement complementary Autism Friendly strategies, as you work together to align them with the inclusionary values of your city and the needs of the residents in your community.

City infrastructure is strengthened when you expand and deepen relationships. The businesses you work with will support you as you support them. A business inclusion program in your city might include the following types of requirements to participate and maintain membership. Training commitments are needed that include an initial introduction to the program and more in-depth workshops about autism. There may be ongoing education throughout the year or when new employees are hired, which can be incorporated into onboarding and orientation. Other conditions might include hiring individuals with autism, or developing pre-employment support, which can be in the form of mentoring, having events such as job shadowing days, or possibly vocational training for people with autism who are interested in a specific career path. It might also include that the businesses participate in volunteering or contributing time to a city task force or community board.

Your city will want to develop ways to acknowledge those partners so that they can be seen and accessed by the community. It is more likely that people in the autism community are will frequent an Autism Friendly Business if given the opportunity. Cities may also want to create a logo, certificate, or window cling that indicates that the business is part of the city's inclusion program.

Autism Acceptance and Awareness Month, Proclamations, and "Light It Up Blue"

There are many ways of celebrating autism awareness in your city. During World Autism Day or Autism Acceptance/Awareness Month in April, many cities will "light it up blue." This means that they will light their city building, a water tower, a bridge, or another prominent or symbolic structure with blue lights to show their support for the autism community. This lighting often goes hand in hand with a ceremony or celebration to highlight the importance of this dedication. This is one very visible way to demonstrate your commitment to the residents in your city with autism.

City leadership has the benefit of creating proclamations, or specialized days and celebrations. Sometimes mayors or city commissioners will even hand out a key to the city. These events are opportunities to recognize individuals with autism and the programs and nonprofits that they participate in or that support them. When hosting autism awareness events, be sure to share your new city initiatives and progress your city is making toward being Autism Friendly.

Another way of increasing autism awareness is to boost the visibility of individuals with autism within your city. For example, when you share stories of city residents or highlight them in a newsletter, be sure to include a diverse representation of people, including those with autism. These could be success stories or perhaps times where your residents are designing new projects or even participating in clubs or classes. When you consider your approach, understand that visibility is important on many levels. The people being included will feel seen and recognized as a member of your city, while other people with autism may feel a kinship or belonging when seeing your city being inclusive, and those without autism or those who have a minimal understanding or knowledge of people with autism will learn more and be reminded that people with all sorts of gifts and neurodifferences live in their community.

Fundraise for Your Program and to Support Others

There are some costs associated with developing and implementing Autism Friendly strategies. Costs can be minimal, but if your city chooses to create a marketing campaign to spread the word, or to remodel a specific space to incorporate a low-sensory room, there may be opportunities to fundraise to support those expenses. Cities may also decide to commit to offer some financial support or fundraising to the organizations that participate on their Inclusion Team.

If your city is planning to fundraise, either for your own programs or to support your local disability nonprofits or community agencies, these are a few ideas and suggestions on how to approach that objective. If you are going to fundraise for a nonprofit, begin by asking what they need, and when they need it. For example, collecting or sponsoring back-to-school supplies and backpacks at the start of a new school year can be a helpful financial and outreach offering. A different option is to determine what month of the year is recognized as their celebration or tribute month. For example, in the United States, April is Autism Acceptance and Awareness Month and April 2nd is World Autism Awareness Day. Other times of the year to celebrate with fundraising might be the annual anniversary of the Americans with Disabilities Act, which takes place in July, or National Disability Employment Month, in October. Events can act as sponsorship and in-kind donations, which might include, in October specifically, a job fair where employers are committed to hire individuals with disabilities, job shadowing for young adults, or employment-related mentoring.

Fundraising for your city might be accomplished in ways that are more traditional, such as a gala with a silent auction, or a 5K run. Other ways of raising funds that also help to improve a city-wide awareness of new initiatives could be to offer city staff opportunities to make a donation in exchange for taking part in a fun activity or a treat. Some cities host a group creativity workshop where the proceeds are donated, or they've had dress-down days where staff get to wear casual attire to work for their donation. Some cities even offer community-based raffles. It may require some technical support internally, but there are cities that have opportunities for employees to engage with charitable donations that come directly out of a pay check, which can be something that is advertised and set up annually. Other groups may offer an opportunity for residents to donate by either having boxes placed around their City Hall area or in some cases if individuals are paying to participate in a program or, for example, a recreational activity; they can round up to the nearest dollar, and the extra amount that they pay becomes a donation to the city's Autism Friendly initiative.

In whichever way you choose to go about fundraising for your own programs, or to support your local organizations and agencies, know that it will be appreciated and is a way to deepen your connection with those who contribute to your initiatives, as well as your residents, sharing how much their time and effort has meaning and that inclusion is an area your city is dedicated to that it is meaningful.

Create a Website or Social Media Page

The only way your community will know that your city is working on Autism Friendly and neurodiverse initiatives is if you tell them. One of the best ways to communicate with your residents is through digital platforms. People come together on social media, utilize apps for navigation and information gathering, and seek solutions from your website. An excellent way to highlight what programs, services, and opportunities you develop is to create an inclusion-specific digital media campaign. Your city may decide to design a unique Autism Friendly or inclusion-specific logo. Some cities work with their marketing departments and develop materials, program names or titles, and press releases. After creating a unique method of showcasing your initiatives, share it across platforms. Be thoughtful about your communication materials to support all your residents in understanding your commitment to inclusion. Include links and information for them to have the chance to participate in new offerings and programs. Also, be sure to work with your Inclusion Team and ask them to share your information throughout their own networks. Keeping these platforms updated with your city's new initiatives, events, and general autism-related information can be useful and informative. Some cities will even create a newsletter for this purpose.

Below you will find website links as examples of digital marketing that exist in the State of Florida at the time of the writing of this book. As you can see, they vary in presentation and how they share information. The cities represented here are the City of Boynton Beach, the City of Tampa, and the City of Miami. Using platforms that directly communicate to your residents is an efficient and effective way to share information. This also creates online resources and replicable models for other cities which might be at the beginning of the Autism Friendly process. It is possible that as you showcase your ideas, solutions, and initiatives to your residents, you may also be helping a city on the other side of the world start their journey.

https://www.boynton-beach.org/accessible-boynton-beach
https://accessmiami.org/
https://www.tampa.gov/accessibility/autism-friendly-tampa

Index

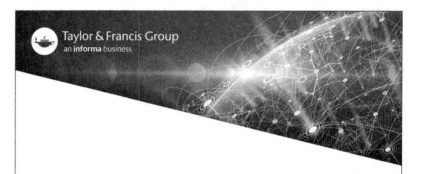

Taylor & Francis eBooks

www.taylorfrancis.com

A single destination for eBooks from Taylor & Francis
with increased functionality and an improved user
experience to meet the needs of our customers.

90,000+ eBooks of award-winning academic content in
Humanities, Social Science, Science, Technology, Engineering,
and Medical written by a global network of editors and authors.

TAYLOR & FRANCIS EBOOKS OFFERS:

A streamlined
experience for
our library
customers

A single point
of discovery
for all of our
eBook content

Improved
search and
discovery of
content at both
book and
chapter level

REQUEST A FREE TRIAL
support@taylorfrancis.com

 Routledge
Taylor & Francis Group

 CRC Press
Taylor & Francis Group

Printed in the United States
by Baker & Taylor Publisher Services